I Have Alot to Say!

D.E. Maddox

ROYSTON
Publishing

BK Royston Publishing
P. O. Box 4321
Jeffersonville, IN 47131
502-802-5385
http://www.bkroystonpublishing.com
bkroystonpublishing@gmail.com

© Copyright – 2021

All Rights Reserved. No part of this book may be reproduced, stored in a retrieval system, or transmitted by any means without the written permission of the author.

Cover Design: Elite Cover Designs
Back Cover Photo: D. E. Maddox

ISBN-13: 978-1-955063-07-4

New King James Version (NKJV)
Scripture taken from the New King James Version®. Copyright © 1982 by Thomas Nelson. Used by permission. All rights reserved.

Printed in the United States of America

James 2: 17–18 reads

"Thus also faith by itself, if it does not have works, is dead. But someone will say, 'You have faith, and I have works.' Show me your faith without works, and I will show you my faith by my works." — NKJV

Table of Contents

Preface — xi

The Poverty Issue — 1

An Incentive for Joining the Military — 7

Lottery Winnings — 9

Forbidding to intermarry is a spiritual issue—not a racial issue. — 15

Affordable Housing in the Newburg Area — 23

Show Idea—Bluegrass Flip — 27

A Prospective Location for a Restaurant — 31

Privacy for Kentucky Lottery Winners — 35

A prospective location for a grocery store — 41

An Angel Tree Idea — 45

A Racist Comment at an Elementary School — 49

Heating and Cooling Scammers — 53

Giving Immigrants the Option to Join the Kentucky National Guard — 55

Creating Stop-and-Talk Zones — 61

Helping the Furloughed Employees — 63

The Bullying Issue	65
An Idea for the Teachers' Pension Fund	71
Getting Rid of Alimony in Kentucky	73
Cool Places to Stay	79
An Ideal Location for More Motels	81
Giving Child Support to Custodial Grandparents	83
Taxing 5% to Bingo Winners	89
Allowing SSI Recipients to Work	91
Clothing for Women with Mastectomies	107
Allowing Non-violent Inmates to Work	109
An Ideal Location for a Drugstore	113
Starting a Statewide Ministers' Convention.	117
Protests near Restaurants	121
Keeping Angel Tree Recipients Safe	129
Have the Casino Work with the Child Support Division.	133
Police Checking Public Parks at Dusk	137
Turning XXXX Poplar Level Road to a Truck Stop	141
Prospective Career Paths for High School Seniors	145

Unsupervised Children Playing in the Street	155
Having Strip Clubs Cooperate with the Child Support Division	159
Transparency on the Ballots	163
Louisville's Surplus Rainy-Day Fund	167
The Grain Farms in Meade County	171
Car Seats and Booster Seats	175
Flash Drives	179
Too Many Logistics Buildings	181
An Idea for a Dollar Store	185
Beware of Dog Signs	191
Busing	193
Court-Ordered Child Support	197
Military People with Work Experience	199
Clothing Stores	203
Vacant Property	205
Studio Apartments	207
School Supplies Donation Boxes	211
Stores Collecting School Supplies	213
Idea for Children in Group Homes	217
A Local Food Bank	219

Free Food Pantry Boxes	221
A Restaurant in a Southeast City	223
To Have One Place to Vote	225
Temperature Pillows	227
A "No Knock" Law	231
Property Managers	233
Stimulus Checks	235
Free Food Box	237
Arcades	241
Ideal Restaurant Location	247
Prospective Drive-In Location	249
Abortions' Impact on Louisville, Kentucky	251
National Right to Life Letter	257
Legalizing Marijuana for Medical Purposes	261
An Idea for the $5 off Purchase Receipts	265
Idea for a Store Manager	267
Having Special Holiday Sales for Entire Month	269
Making People Order Services in Person	273
Setting Up a Free Food/Book Box	281

Trees in Jeopardy of Falling During an Ice Storm	285
People Feeling Intimidated about Receiving Food from Food Boxes.	287
Putting Speed Bumps on our Streets.	289
YOU'RE GONE AWAY	291
Epilogue	293
About the Author	295

Preface

I have written letters to people in office since the late 1990's or early 2000's. When I was younger, I used to complain about everything going on. My paternal grandmother looked at me one day and asked, "And what are you doing about it?!" My jaw dropped. She then said, "Besides complaining about everything, what are you doing about it?!" My question to myself became "What am I doing about it?"

I wrote letters to presidents and vice presidents of the United States. I wrote letters to First Ladies and vice presidents' wives. I wrote letters to Louisville mayors and Kentucky governors. I even wrote letters to council people, senators and representatives. I also wrote letters to CEO's and managers of big companies. If I have an idea, then I share it with somebody. The rule I learned to live by is, "If I have an idea and don't have the power to do anything about it, then share the idea with somebody who does."

I believe God fills my head with ideas because He knows I will share the ideas with others. If I do not share all my ideas with others, then I might go crazy!

I never share ideas about how to make my life better. Instead, I share ideas about how to improve all our lives. For example, I will never write a letter about turning the empty lot near my house to a store so it can benefit me. Instead, I might write a letter about how turning an empty store front or a vacant building in our neighborhood to an afterschool place for the children in my neighborhood.

I started to save my letters on my USB drive back in 2014. I want to share with you the letters I have written as well as some of the response letters I have received. (The letters in this book have been gently edited for consistency and punctuation.)

Some of the letters in this book are not suitable for children to read.

Some letters you might agree with and others you might not. Also, not all people in office agree with what I have to say. For example, I wrote a letter suggesting that 5 percent of gambling revenues (such as the lottery, the casino, and bingo halls) be used toward replenishing the Teachers' Pension Fund. A person in office (identity I choose to not reveal) said it was a ridiculous idea. This person in office got on local TV and said, "The idea of using casino money to replenish the Teachers' Pension Fund is the most ridiculous idea I've ever heard."

It is good to have faith and believe things will improve and get better. We also need to add works to our faith. My writing is my "works" and I use it to share concerns, ideas, and suggestions.

This is a letter I wrote on July 7, 2014, and I sent it to a few people in office. I do not remember whether I have received a response from anybody.

The Poverty Issue

Dear _____:

It was brought to my attention that many celebrities and politicians have been trying to create solutions for the poverty issue in America. I can say, from personal experience, that one of many factors pertaining to the poverty issue here in the United States is that too many people are waiting for somebody else to get them out of poverty.

I have three examples of how some people choose to wait for somebody else to rescue them and get them out of poverty.

Scenario #1

There are ladies who have children by a man (or men) who never marry them. The woman then sits up in poverty waiting for a rich man or military man or some other kind of financially secure man to marry her so that he can get her children and her out of poverty. To make things worse, some of these ladies die waiting. If all of us females make this kind of choice, then some women would <u>never</u> become "First Ladies" or doctors or lawyers or governors or educators or inventors or scientists and so on.

Scenario #2

Some people are too busy playing the "blame game" when it comes to their circumstances. For example, a former fiancé of mine blames me for why the mother of two of his children had to raise her five children in poverty since I never found her a rich husband. To make the situation worse, it was brought to my attention that his children needing clothes and shoes was my fault for not doing my Christian job right. In other words, if I were a true Christian, then I would have money to buy clothes and shoes for all the poor children in my community and put money into the hands of poor mothers. Since I do not have the financial means to buy clothes and shoes for all the poor children and give money to poor mothers, then I am not a true Christian and I am going to hell on Judgment Day (according to him).

Scenario #3

Too many people are trying to create "Wealth Without Work" schemes. For one example, there are fathers who hope the mothers of their children find rich husbands. Afterward, the rich husband is supposed to die, and the mother is supposed to split her rich late husband's money with the birthfather (or birthfathers) of her children. (This is wishful thinking as far as the birthfathers are concerned.)

Way back in 2000, my former fiancé was one of many men who tried this. In fact, I was criticized and condemned for not finding a rich husband for the mother of two of his children. He even holds me at fault for why the mother of his children raised all her children in poverty because I never found her a rich husband. A few years later, I had a dream I found a rich husband for the mother of his children and the rich husband ended up killed by getting shot in the head. After the wife inherited her dead husband's money, she split the money with the father (or fathers) of her children. (I am glad that dream never came true.) Because of that dream, I decided that if my inability to find rich husbands for poor, single mothers continue to get me blamed for single mothers raising children in poverty, then I will gladly endure the blame.

As far as poverty in the United States is concerned, some of the many factors are as follows: A single mother sitting in poverty waiting for a financially secure man to marry her; Too many people blaming others for their situations instead of doing something for their children as well as themselves; Or too many people who have some kind of "Wealth Without Work" Scheme.

Job creativity is a wonderful thing, but we cannot make people work if they are too lazy and too busy blaming others for their impoverished situations. I wish there was a law against laziness—but there isn't.

I hope that celebrities and politicians as well as other leaders can encourage people to work toward getting themselves out of poverty. In other words, get themselves out of their impoverished situations and stop blaming others for their poverty.

Please create speeches that would motivate people to get up and work instead of waiting for somebody else to get them out of poverty or blame others for their situations or try to create some kind of "Wealth Without Work" scheme. Also, let us motivate ladies to do for themselves and stop waiting for some man to marry her and get her out of poverty!

Thank you for reading my letter. I deeply appreciate it.

I wrote this letter on September 15, 2014. I remember mailing copies to the president and vice president of the United States. I received a response, but I never kept the letter.

An Incentive for Joining the Military

Dear _____:

Hello. I have an idea. The United States military is severely short-staffed, so my idea is to give young people an incentive for joining the military. Military persons who are under 21 should be entitled to buy alcoholic beverages while they are physically enlisted in the military. Of course, they would be required to follow the same laws as everybody else when it comes to alcoholic beverages such as never drive while intoxicated and to never be publicly intoxicated. Maybe this would bring up the recruitment rate. If an individual is old enough to die for our country, then they should be entitled to buy alcoholic beverages as lang as they are physically enlisted while under 21 and so long as they abide by the laws of the land such as not driving while intoxicated, and so on.

I hope the idea of allowing military personal under 21 to purchase alcoholic beverages if they abide by the laws pertaining to alcoholic beverages could be considered. If they are old enough to fight for this country, then they should be entitled to incentives such as the privilege to purchase alcoholic beverages so long they drink responsibility.

I want to thank you for reading my letter. I deeply appreciate it.

I wrote this letter on August 29, 2014. I believe I wrote and mailed this letter to the president and vice president of the United States.

Lottery Winnings

Dear _____:

I am writing about a concern and an idea. In the past, there have been incidences in which a non-custodial parent is not paying their court-ordered child support to the custodial parent even when the non-custodial parent wins the lottery. After the non-custodial parent wins the lottery, they continue to not pay their child support and/or their backpay. To make things worse, they would win the lottery in another state and the custodial parent (or guardian) never knows about it and never receives any of the deeply needed money. For example, a man could owe thousands of dollars in child support in Kentucky but win the $250 million Powerball in Wisconsin. I feel that there should be a federal law that requires lottery officials throughout North America to see if the lottery winners owe child support in any state or U.S. territory. If so, then the money is to be used for present payments as well as backpay. I hope you can create a federal law stating that lottery winnings will be distributed among the custodial parents (or guardians) before the non-custodial parent gets any of the money if the lottery winner owes court-ordered child support anywhere in the United States.

If the non-custodial parent cries, "Not fair!" then I will tell them what is not fair. It is unfair for children to face another winter without warm clothes while the non-custodial parent gets to go on shopping sprees. It is unfair for children to go days without eating while the non-custodial parent eats at the best restaurants. It is unfair for children to wear high-water pants, shoes with holes in them, and tattered clothes while the non-custodial parent gets to splurge their lottery winnings on travel, vacations, entertainment, strip clubs, and so on. It is unfair for children and their custodial parents (or guardians) to depend on public transportation while the non-custodial parent gets to drive in style in his or her new car.

It is only fair if portions if the lottery winnings go toward the custodial parent (or guardian) first. The non-custodial parent should learn to make do with the "left-overs." Many non-custodial parents are able-bodied adults who can work to provide for themselves. If they are old enough to buy lottery tickets, then they can get jobs so they can provide for themselves. Small children cannot work to provide for themselves.

My concern is about the non-custodial parents who are wanted in one state for not paying child support but win the lottery in another state and the money is never collected on behalf of the custodial parent (or guardian). My idea is to create a federal law that requires searching all 50 states as well as U.S. territories to see if the lottery winner owes child support anywhere. The portion of the money will be distributed among the custodial parents (or guardians) before the lottery winner receives his or her share of the winnings. Maybe, a red flag can show up on the computer screen if the lottery winner owes child support anywhere in North America.

When the non-custodial parents who are lottery winners are made to render a portion of their winnings to the custodial parents (or guardians), then the children will be able to have what they need. The children will finally receive the clothes and shoes they need. The children will have food to eat every day. Also, their parents (or guardians) might be able to have a safe and reliable form of transportation. The deeply needed financial support could bring forth many other positive outcomes.

I hope that the idea to make it a federal law for all lottery winners who owe court-ordered child support as well as backpay to have to use a portion of their winnings to pay their court-ordered child support regardless of what state they are in can be considered. If a man wins the $100 million lottery in Hawaii, but owes child support in Puerto Rico, then the mother (or mothers) in Puerto Rico will receive a fair share of the money. If a woman owes child support in New York State and she wins $200 million in Kentucky, then she should be required to pay a portion to the father (or fathers) in New York State.

Thank you for reading my letter. I deeply appreciate it.

---

*I received a response, but I never kept the letter. (frown)

In 2018, I started to save all my letters to USB drive as well as the response letters.

Here is a letter I wrote on August 9, 2018, to a well-known evangelistic association.

Forbidding to intermarry is a spiritual issue—not a racial issue.

To Whom It May Concern:

I am going to be 50 in October, and I am writing with a serious concern. I am racially mixed because I have a Black father and a White mother. I have been judged, condemned, and ridiculed practically my entire life due to this. I now live in a predominantly Black community in Louisville, Kentucky, and some people here are against women mixed with Black and White ever getting married. I had my suspicions for years, and I asked the Lord, "If this is true, then please allow me to hear it from somebody else." A few years later, I was having a phone conversation with a Puerto Rican man who lives in West Louisville and he said to me, "The people in your neighborhood don't want people mixed with Black and White to ever get married." I was shocked! The people in my community are Church-going folks. But my question is: what are they learning in church? For example, when God instructed His people to not intermarry it was a spiritual issue—not a racial one. Deuteronomy 7:3–4 reads, "³Neither shalt thou make marriages with them; thy daughter thou shalt not give unto his son, nor his daughter shalt thou take onto thy son. ⁴For they will turn away thy son from following me, that they may serve other gods: so will the anger of the Lord be kindled against you, and destroy thee suddenly." (KJV) 2 Corinthians 6:14 reads, "Be ye not unequally yoked together with unbelievers: for what fellowship hath righteousness with unrighteousness? and what communion hath light with darkness?" (KJV) These are all indications that to not intermarry was a spiritual issue and not a racial issue. I wish churches all over the world will start teaching this.

There are those who forbid me to marry, and they invent stupid reasons for why I am unworthy of marriage. Some people say they cannot marry me because I do not have a college degree. I have German ancestry on my mother's side of the family and others say they cannot marry me because of my German ancestry. (Both a Black man and a White man have told me this at different times in the past.) At least two Black men have decided that my inability to fulfill the need of poor, Black children and their poor, single Black mothers makes me unworthy of him. The second man decided that my inability to buy clothes and shoes for all the poor, Black children; give money to poor, single Black mothers; and find rich, Black husbands for poor, single Black mothers makes me guilty for Black mothers raising their children in poverty and a suitable "punishment" is no husband. **That makes no sense!** If a man does not want to marry me (or get married at all) then he should tell the truth and say so. My major concern is that my getting married can lead to bad consequences for my family and me. To make matters worse, those who carry out the bad consequences are those who grew up in the Church and call themselves "Christians." 1 Timothy 4:1–3 reads, "[1]Now the Spirit speaketh expressly, that in the latter times some shall depart from the faith, giving heed to seductive spirits, and doctrine of devils; [2]Speaking lies in hypocrisy; having their conscience seared with a hot iron;

[3]**Forbidding to marry**, and commending to abstain from meats, which God hath created to be received with thanksgiving of them which believe and know the truth." (KJV emphasis is mine) The point is: to forbid me to marry a man for any lame (or racial) reason is evil. If a man is a

single, divorced, or widowed Christian man, then why can we not get married?

The point is: when the Bible instructs those to not "intermarry" or "be unequally yoked," it is a spiritual issue and not a racial issue. If a Black man and White woman who are both born-again Christians want to marry each other, then let them. If a Korean man wants to marry a Black woman and they are both born-again Christians, then allow them to do so.

Thanks for reading my letter. I deeply appreciate it.

I received a response letter from this evangelistic association on August 16, 2018.

Dear Dorothea:

Thank you for writing to us about your concerns related to those who would speak out against interracial marriage.

We find nothing stated in the Bible that would prohibit someone from dating or marrying a member of a different race. The idea of "staying with your own tribe" is not supported Biblically, even though the Old Testament law commanded the Jews to not intermarry with other races (Deuteronomy 7:3–4). The reason for the command was God's knowledge that the Jews would be led astray from His true worship if they intermarried with pagan idol worshippers. Consequently, the command was not in consideration of racial differences but of spiritual incompatibility.

Scripture mentions several marriages between Israelites and Gentiles, who chose to follow the true God (Numbers 12:1, Ruth 4:13, Matthew 1:5). Intertribal marriages were clearly possible, though properly could not be transferred between tribes (Numbers, chapter 36).

The most important issue regarding dating and marriage relations is spiritual, not racial. In

2 Corinthians 6:14 we read, "Do not be yoked together with unbelievers. For what do righteousness and wickedness have in common?"

We encourage you to seek the council of your pastor or a local gospel-preaching pastor for additional guidance on this and other biblical or spiritual questions. They should be able to provide more ongoing, personal counsel for you.

You have been remembered in prayer. May the Lord bless and encourage you today. "The Lord gives strength to his people; the Lord blesses his people with peace." (Psalm 29:11, NIV).

*Some changes were made from the original letter.

I wrote and mailed this letter to the Louisville mayor on August 20, 2018.

Affordable Housing in the Newburg Area

Dear Mayor _____:

I am writing with a concern and an idea. My concern is about the lack of affordable housing in Newburg. My idea is to build the same kind of affordable housing that they have in Downtown Louisville, West Louisville, and South Louisville. For example, there was an apartment for rent in Downtown Louisville (off Eastern Parkway) and the rent was $170 per week— this also covers utilities). Also, something is being built on Shepherdsville Road (between Rangeland Road and Poplar Level Road). Residents around Newburg are hoping that It is affordable housing like the kind in Downtown Louisville, West Louisville, and South Louisville. To have affordable housing will benefit those who work in the Park Jefferson areas. My place of employment is in Park Jefferson, Entrance #2, and we are next to the 6th Division Police Department. Many employees drive from as far as Nelson County, Hardin County and Bullitt County. To have affordable housing at this location would also benefit those who work in the Jefferson Boulevard Industrial Area as well at those who work at General Electric. (Just because a person works at General Electric does not mean that they have an unlimited cash flow.)

To build affordable housing on Shepherdsville Road (between Rangeland Road and Poplar Level Road) will benefit those who have jobs on the #43 Poplar Level Road and the #62 Breckinridge Lane bus routes. Many people do not have vehicles due to financial limitations, so they must take the bus everywhere. Also, many young people are looking to become self-sufficient and many middle-aged people like me are looking to become self-sufficient again. I lost my house on Ilex Avenue many, many years ago due to my allowing a poor, single mother and her three small boys to move into my house. It was more than my finances can handle due to my being the only one in the house working. To make matters worse, the poor, single mother was high maintenance. For example, her children and she were to never eat food from "Dare to Care." They were to <u>only</u> eat food bought from a grocery store. They say, "Don't be high maintenance if you're poor!" (Or "beggars cannot be choosers" although they try to be). Her high standards caused me to go into debt as far as cash loans are concerned and I eventually lost everything.

To allow the Shepherdsville Road Area (between Rangeland Road and Poplar Level Road) to become affordable housing will benefit those who work in: Park Jefferson; General Electric; and the Jefferson Boulevard Industrial Sites. To have affordable housing in this area would also benefit all of those who have jobs on the #43 Poplar Level Road and the #62 Breckinridge Lane bus lines.

I hope that to have affordable housing built on Shepherdsville Road (between Rangeland Road and Poplar Level Road) would be discussed and taken into consideration.

Thank you for reading my letter. I deeply appreciate it.

*I have never received a response from this letter.

*I deliberately left out the name of the mayor to protect his identity.

This letter was written and mailed on September 5, 2018. I have written this letter to a national home network studio, the Kentucky governor, and a statewide TV studio.

Show Idea—Bluegrass Flip

Dear _____:

I am writing with an idea. There are abandoned houses throughout Kentucky. Also, according to statistics, Kentucky has the highest inmate population in the South. My idea is to create a television show called, "Bluegrass Flip." During the spring and summer months, inmates throughout Kentucky can receive free job training while helping to rebuild and restore abandoned houses. The inmates will work on these houses while under the strict supervision of experienced and certified house builders. The inmates will learn electrical installation while under the supervision of experienced and certified electricians. The inmates will learn how to install plumbing while under the supervision of experienced and certified plumbers. Of course, they will also be under the strict supervision of armed security guards.

To have a show called "Bluegrass Flip" can bring job training to those who need it the most. It can also bring restoration to houses throughout Kentucky. When people buy these restored houses, the inmates are to never know who purchased the homes. For example, if an attractive, middle-aged widow buys a restored house and she lives alone, then it would not be wise to allow male inmates to know about it. In other words, the identities of those who buy the restored houses will remain anonymous as far as the inmates are concerned.

(I gave the mailing address to the studio. But I choose to not reveal the mailing address without the studio's permission).

I hope that the idea of having a show called "Bluegrass Flip" can be discussed and taken into consideration.

Thank you for reading my letter. I deeply appreciate it.

*Changes were made from the original letter.

Here is the response letter I have received from the Kentucky governor.

Dear Ms. Maddox:

Thank you for taking time to contact the governor's office. The governor is committed to providing servant leadership during his administration and he recognizes that moving the commonwealth forward requires a team effort. Our administration appreciates your useful comments and suggestions. I have made the governor aware of your suggestion.

This letter is to confirm receipt of your correspondence, and to let you know that I have forwarded it to the appropriate staff member for review.

Sincerely,

Director of Constituent Services

*Changes were made to this letter. Names of people In office I choose to not reveal.

I wrote this letter a multiple restaurant franchises to help put a restaurant at a vacant location in my neighborhood. It was written and mailed on October 13, 2018.

A Prospective Location for a Restaurant

Dear_____:

I am writing with an idea. There is a prospective location in the Newburg neighborhood of Louisville, Kentucky for a restaurant. (Location of building and Realtors I choose to not reveal.)

The former restaurant was recently shut down. A company tried to buy the property and turn it into a liquor store. Many people in my community (including some of my relatives) fought to keep another liquor store out of our neighborhood. I hope to see something positive in this location. To have a restaurant in this location would bring job creativity to our community as well as give people in our community a low-costing restaurant to come to for a quick and convenient meal. Many people in our community are low-income to middle-income working people. To have a place with low-costing menu items would be a tremendous blessing to many of the people in our community.

Finding employees would be easy for three reasons:

#1—This location is walking distance from many homes.

#2—This location is on a bus line.

#3—This location would be a short drive for many prospective employees who have vehicles.

I hope the idea to putting a restaurant in our neighborhood can be discussed and considered.

Thank you for reading my letter. I deeply appreciate it.

*I have received responses from a few restaurant franchises, but not all of them.

*I have kept a copy of USB drive and mailed this letter on different occasions.

*Changes were made from the original letter.

Here is a response letter I received from a pizza chain franchise in Ohio on October 28, 2019.

Dear Ms. Maddox,

Thank you for your taking your time to share your interest of having our restaurant join your community.

Currently, our restaurant in not building in this area.

We will keep this location information on file and hope to be in the Louisville market someday soon.

Sincerely,

I wrote this letter to the Kentucky governor. It was written on October 20, 2018. It was mailed on October 22, 2018.

I copied this same letter from my USB drive and mailed copies to both my state senator and my state representative on June 5, 2019.

Privacy for Kentucky Lottery Winners

Dear Governor_____:

I am writing with a concern and an idea. My concern is how some people who win the lottery feel intimidated about coming forward. My idea is to allow those who win the lottery in Kentucky to keep their identities a secret. For example, if Mrs. LeeAnn McCoy (fictional person) in Eastern Kentucky wins the lottery and she happens to be a widow, then the only thing the news reporters can say is, "An elderly widow in Eastern Kentucky is the latest lottery winner." Nobody needs to know the winner was Mrs. LeeAnn McCoy.

Before the national lottery reached $1 billion, my coworkers and I all started a lottery pool. If we win, then the only thing the news reporters would be allowed to say is, "A group of employees at a logistics facility in Louisville, Kentucky, are the latest lottery winners."

My father and mother work at facilities in East Louisville. My mother's workplace also had a lottery pool. If they win the lottery, then the only thing the news reporters can say is, "A group of Kentucky employees who work at a facility in East Louisville are the latest lottery winners." In other words, neither identities nor workplaces would be revealed. Only the part of the city or state can be identified.

I am aware that when a person wins the lottery (especially the Mega Millions) then they are required to reveal their identities. This can put the lottery winners' lives in danger, as well as the lives of their relatives. For example, if I win millions in this lottery pool, then there are those in my city who would hurt some of my family members just to get my lottery winnings. If I decide to take my lottery winnings and move to Crete, Greece (where I lived as a child when my father was in the Air Force), then my family members could get hurt as my "punishment" for not giving these specific people my lottery winnings. Even if I give these specific people my lottery winnings, then they can still do something to my family. There have been stories of somebody kidnapping a person's children (or grandchildren) for ransom. The family gives the kidnappers the money and the children still end up getting killed.

If Kentucky becomes the first and only state to allow lottery winners to keep their identities private, then people from other states might "flock" to our state to buy their lottery tickets due to our "Right to Privacy" law when it comes to winning the lottery. If people from Ohio, West Virginia, Indiana, Illinois, Missouri, Tennessee, and Virginia drive to Kentucky to buy their tickets, then this can boost our economy as well as add money to Kentucky's higher education programs.

I hope the idea of allowing lottery winners in Kentucky the option of keeping their identities a secret can be discussed and considered.

Thank you for reading my letter. I deeply appreciate it.

This is the response letter from the Kentucky governor. It was written on October 24, 2018. I received it on October 26, 2018.

Dear Ms. Maddox:

Thank you for taking the time to contact me, and I appreciate your input. Moving the Commonwealth forward requires a team effort. As we strive to bring the best opportunities to Kentuckians across the state, your comments and suggestions are welcome and very useful. I am committed to providing servant leadership during my administration and dedicated to establishing open and honest dialogue with every Kentuckian.

As citizens, we should take sour state motto to heart: "United We Stand, Divided We Fall." Together, we must take pride in our Commonwealth. Although there will be challenges in the years to come, with the help of citizens like you, we can make Kentucky the greatest version of itself. United, we can shore up Kentucky's workforce, reinvest in infrastructure, and make Kentucky the crown jewel in the manufacturing sector. By working together, we can create a Kentucky that shines like a beacon for the entire world to see and emulate.

It is an honor to serve as your governor and I look forward to your continued feedback. Please do not hesitate to contact me in the future on any matter of importance to you.

I wrote and mailed this letter on October 23, 2018.

A prospective location for a grocery store

To Whom It May Concern:

I am writing with a concern and an idea. I have an aunt who lives in Bloomfield, Kentucky, and the town no longer has a grocery store. All the residents must drive 12 miles to Bardstown to buy their groceries. To make matters worse, some residents do not have vehicles and depend on others to give them rides to the grocery stores in Bardstown. My idea is for your company to put a grocery store in the middle of town.

(Location of former store I choose to not reveal).

(Name of Real Estate Agents I choose to not reveal).

I hope to see a grocery store in Bloomfield, Kentucky, soon.

Thank you for reading my letter. I deeply appreciate it.

*I have received a response from at least two grocery store franchises.

*I have put copies on my USB drive and sent letters to multiple grocery franchises.

I received a letter from one franchise, which was written on October 30, 2018. I received it on November 5, 2018.

Dear Ms. Maddox,

Thank you for contacting us.

Our grocery store franchise (name I choose to not reveal) is always looking for new geographical areas to continue to bring smart shoppers the highest quality products at the lowest possible prices. While we have a lot of criteria for choosing store locations, our No. 1 reason is to be where our grocery store franchise fans are shopping. We appreciate your positive feedback, and your locations suggestion will be shared with our real estate team.

Thank you again for your interest in our grocery store franchise.

Kind regards,

Grocery store franchise Customer Service

Here is a letter received from a second grocery store franchise. The letter was written on December 8, 2018. I received it on December 13, 2018.

Dear Dorothea Maddox,

Thank you for taking the time to contact us. We value our customers and welcome their feedback.

Thank you for inviting us to locate a store in Bloomfield, KY! You can reach out to our Real Estate Department to suggest a new location. (Name, phone number and website address I choose to not reveal.)

If we can be of further assistance in the future, please contact us.

Sincerely,

Corporate Customer Care

This letter was written and mailed on November 17, 2018. I wrote this letter to the mayor of Louisville as well as a national charity organization.

Since I kept a copy on my USB drive, I mailed copies to both my senator and representative on May 28, 2019.

An Angel Tree Idea

Dear _____:

I am writing with an idea pertaining to the Angel Tree Program. I moved to Louisville in 1985 when I was a teenager and I have noticed that all the angels on angel trees were either Black or White. It was also brought to my attention that ever since the 1970's, Louisville was becoming a "melting pot" when it comes to racial diversity. Way back in the 1990's, when I used to sign my daughter up for the Angel Tree Program, I also noticed that many recipients were Black, White, Hispanic, Asian, Arabic, and

Native American. Due to the "rich" racial diversity of our city, the angels on angel trees should not be either Black or White.

My idea is to make the angels on angel tree color coded.

Possible example:

Girl Angels=pink

Boy Angels=light blue

Angels for infant girls=lavender

Angels for infant boys=peach

I do not know if you can start this idea this year, but I hope to see this idea being put into practice for Christmas of 2019.

I also believe that it is not a good idea to make the angels on the angel tree a certain race because of the growing population of racially mixed people. Many of today's children are mixed with: Black and White; Black and Hispanic; White and Hispanic; Black and Asian; White and Asian; Black and Arabic; White and Arabic; Black and Italian; and so on. The point is: this city does not consist of only Blacks and Whites so why should the angel tree angel be only Black or White?

I hope the idea of making the angels on angel trees color coded can be discussed and taken into consideration.

Thank you for reading my letter. I deeply appreciate it.

What Do You Want To Say?

I wrote this letter on December 9, 2018. I mailed it on December 10, 2018, to the Louisville mayor and the public school superintendent.

A Racist Comment at an Elementary School

Dear _____:

There was a conversation at my job that was very disturbing. A Black coworker told me that her 5-year-old granddaughter's Art Teacher told her that all White people hate Blacks. This is a lie, and no teacher should be allowed to teach this to children. My father is Black, and my mother is White. My twin brother and my paternal aunt even have photos of both my maternal and paternal grandparents at the table and conversing with each other. (I simply do not know which elementary school it occurred at.)

All Jefferson County Public School Teachers need to be retrained and be required to take diversity classes. Racist comments and stereotypes should never be accepted in our public school systems. As a mixed person, I have dealt with hatred come at me from both sides. Some Black people accused me of hating Blacks due to my fair skin, European facial features, hair texture, and my having long hair. Some White people accused me of hating Whites due to my tan skin and course hair texture. I have had a terrible life due to racist stereotypes.

Thank you for reading my letter.

*Some changes were made from the original letter.

This is the letter I have received from the mayor of Louisville:

Ms. Maddox:

Thank you for your letter regarding anti-racism training for all teachers employed by Jefferson County Public Schools. Though the Mayor's Office does not control JCPS, we are happy to share your concern with their Diversity, Equity, and Poverty Division. We know that the JCPS central office is dedicated to creating a climate where every student feels valued and where intolerance is simply not tolerated.

I will ask that a JCPS representative reach out to you directly.

Thank you.

Sincerely,

Senior Advisor to the Mayor

* A few changes were made to this letter.

* A JCPS representative called me on my cell phone.

I wrote this letter to a local heating and cooling (HVAC) Company.

Heating and Cooling Scammers

To Whom It May Concern:

It was brought to my attention by a neighbor that a couple is going around bingo halls hanging up bogus business cards and telling others they work for your company. A man who rents a house called the couple to his house to fix his air conditioner. The couple came out and inspected the air conditioner. They told him it would cost $3,000. The man was about to go to the bank to take out a $3,000 loan, but he decided to call the property manager first. The property manager came out, checked out the air conditioner and discovered that it only needed a $5.00 piece. The property manager also had the piece in his truck he needed to fix the air conditioner.

My concern is knowing these "imposters" who claimed to work for your company might have scammed many people out of money! Who knows? The scammers can damage your company's reputation. My idea is to have employees check the bingo halls from time to time to be sure these "imposters" are not still hanging up bogus business cards and approaching others claiming to work for your company. Another idea is to create a commercial allowing the public to know the dos and don'ts when it comes to allowing people to come to their house to fix anything. Thanks in advance.

Thank you for reading my letter. I deeply appreciate it.

*I choose to not reveal the HVAC company's name.

*Some changes were made to the letter.

This letter was written and mailed to the Kentucky governor on July 26, 2019.

Giving Immigrants the Option to Join the Kentucky National Guard

Dear Governor_____:

I am writing with an idea. I know that Kentucky receives a lot of immigrants from Mexico, Central America, South America, Europe, Africa, Canada, and Australia. My idea is to allow the young adults (depending on age and health) to join the Kentucky National Guard for three years in order to obtain their citizenship more quickly. While in the Kentucky National Guard they will spend their first year in basic training as well as learning to read, write and speak American English. After the first year, they will receive training in areas of deepest need here in Kentucky. For example, Kentucky is in desperate need Nationally Certified

Pharmacy Technicians so some of them will receive the education and training necessary to become a Nationally Certified Pharmacy Technician. Other areas they can be trained in are X-Ray technician, ultrasound technician, dental assistant, veterinary technician, diesel repair technician, Class A CDL drivers, and other careers. For those who want to stay in the Army for 5 to 10 years can receive options of becoming nurses, morticians, pharmacists, and so on. Those who want to stay in the Army for 10 years or more can receive the education and training necessary to become family doctors, surgeons, pediatricians, urologists, gynecologists, and so on.

This is a compromise: We give them a free and easy way to become legal American citizens as well as the opportunity to gain extremely important job skills. They then become the working-class and tax-paying citizens that Kentucky needs. As a result, Kentucky soon will have more doctors, surgeons, school teachers, pharmacists, nurses, morticians, Class A CDL drivers, and so on, who are deeply needed by our state.

I hope the idea of allowing immigrants to join the Kentucky Nation Guard as an easy way of gaining their citizenship can be discussed and taken into consideration.

Thank you for reading my letter. I deeply appreciate it.

* I do not remember receiving a response letter.

I wrote this letter to some clothing store and department store franchises. It was written and mailed on July 29, 2019.

To Whom It May Concern:

I am writing with a suggestion. There are many women who have had mastectomies due to breast cancer and some of them either cannot afford implants or choose to not get them. My suggestion is for your company to come up with a selection of clothing for women in these situations—including swimsuits. I know a woman who cannot find an affordable swimsuit for somebody who has had a mastectomy. Also, many women feel like she is "less than a woman" after the surgery. I hope your company can come out with both undergarments and outerwear that make women in these situations feel like they are women again.

I hope you can come up with a line of clothing for women who have had mastectomies and need prosthetics. Please help women in this situation feel like women again. Thanks in advance.

Thank you for reading my letter. I deeply appreciate it.

*I do not remember receiving a response to this letter.

I wrote and mailed this letter on January 12, 2019. I mailed copies to both the Kentucky governor and the Louisville mayor.

I made copies of this letter from my USB drive and mailed copies to both my state senator and my state representative on June 5, 2019.

Creating Stop-and-Talk Zones

Dear _____:

I am writing with an idea. My idea is to establish Stop-and-Talk Zones throughout the state/city. There are abandoned houses that have not been lived in for more than 15 or 20 years. If nobody is interested in the house, then tear down the house, fill the vacant area with gravel and set a "Stop-and-Talk" sign at the end of the graveled area.

I got the idea for establishing Stop-and-Talk zones while I was driving down the road here in Louisville. I was pulling into a subdivision when I got a call on my mobile phone. I pulled into a graveled area, parked my car, checked my phone, and then returned the call. The point is: I was safe, and I kept the other drivers on the road safe. All the Stop-and-Talk zones will be used for making phone calls, answering phone calls, making texts, answering texts and so on.

I hope the idea of establishing Stop-and-Talk Zones throughout the city/state can be discussed and taken into consideration.

Thank you for reading my letter. I deeply appreciate it.

This letter was written and mailed on January 23, 2019. I have mailed copies to both the Kentucky governor and the Louisville mayor.

Helping the Furloughed Employees

Dear _____:

I have an idea pertaining to helping all the furloughed employees in our state/city. My idea is to have 5% of all monies gained through the Kentucky Lottery donated to all furloughed employees. For example, every $1 I spend on a lottery ticket a nickel will be donated to furloughed employees. Kentucky/Louisville makes millions each month in lottery ticket sales. If Kentucky/Louisville makes $100 million in revenue due to the lottery, then $5 million will go to pay the furloughed employees. Also, all winners need to agree to allow 5% of their winnings to be donated for furloughed employees. For example, if I win $300 on a scratch-off, then $15 will be donated toward helping furloughed employees throughout the state/city. The Kentucky Lottery Headquarters is to post a sign on all machines stating that "5% of money going into the machine will be donated to furloughed employees. Also, 5% of what you win will go toward furloughed employees throughout the state/city." If I win $1,000 that means $50 will go towards furloughed employees in our state/city.

I hope this idea can be discussed and considered.

Thank you for reading my letter. I deeply appreciate it.

I also wrote and mailed this letter on January 23, 2019. This letter was also mailed to both the Kentucky governor and Louisville mayor.

The Bullying Issue

Dear _____:

I am writing with a concern and an idea pertaining to bullying. My concern is the fact that bullying can get to the extreme in which people are committing suicide because of it. My idea is to hold all adults in the school system accountable for school bullying. That includes all school principals, all assistant principals, all school teachers, all substitute teachers, all custodians, all cafeteria employees, all bus drivers, all bus monitors, all librarians, and all other school employees. When my father completed his assignment in Fort Ord, California, my twin brother, and I spent the second semester of our first-grade year here in

Louisville (before our father was assigned to Okinawa, Japan), and we went to an elementary school here. The other children beat me up on a regular basis and the teacher just watched. I looked at her one day and begged her to make them stop, but she just stood there and shrugged her shoulders. Did she allow the other children to beat me up because I am mixed? I have a Black father and a White mother. Was I the victim of both racism and bullying? The point is: school bullying has occurred for decades and nobody is being held accountable.

My idea is to hold all adults in a school system accountable. If a child comes to an adult to say that he or she is being bullied, then the adult is required to do something about it. If a child sees another child being bullied and he or she tells an adult, then the adult is required to do something. In other words, somebody better do something!

The myth about bullying is that it only happens to preteen and teenagers. This is a lie! People of all ages can be the victims of bullying! I was the victim of bullying during my preteen and teen years, as well as during my 20's and 30's. I have all kinds of stories that others will never believe occurred, but they did!

All of us are to be held accountable for bullying! For example, If I see an older Muslim woman being teased and humiliated in public because of her attire, then it is my obligation to react and defend her. My doing nothing would also make me guilty. To make matters worse: too many people are videoing people being bullied and posting these incidences on social media. All those who do this should be banned from social media for a year. If they have too many offenses, then they should be banned for life. These laws sound tough, but if I were a lawmaker, then I would put these laws into effect if it would prevent and eliminate bullying.

Many bullies know people will video them and put them on social media and that is why they are doing the bullying. People who do this need to stop rewarding bullies! People who post incidences of bullying on social media are also accountable. They are guilty of "rewarding" bullies by putting them on social media beating another person up. Doing this should also be a criminal offense. Never "reward" bullies!

I hope all my ideas can be discussed and taken into consideration.

Thank you for reading my letter. I deeply appreciate it.

This letter was written on behalf of the Kentucky governor on January 29, 2019. I received it on January 31, 2019.

Dear Ms. Maddox:

Thank you for taking the time to contact me, and I appreciate your input. Moving the Commonwealth forward requires a team effort. As we strive to bring the best opportunities to Kentuckians across the state, your comments and suggestions are welcome and very useful. I am committed to providing servant leadership during my administration and dedicated to establishing open and honest dialogue with every Kentuckian.

As citizens, we should take our state motto to heart: "United We Stand, Divided We Fall." Together, we must take pride in our Commonwealth. Although there will be challenges in the years to come, with the help of citizens like you, we can make Kentucky the greatest version of itself. United, we can shore up Kentucky's workforce, reinvest in infrastructure, and make Kentucky the crown jewel in the manufacturing sector. By working together, we can create a Kentucky that shines like a beacon for the entire work to see and emulate.

It is an honor to serve as your governor and I look forward to your continued feedback. Please do not hesitate to contact me in the future on any matter of importance to you.

    Sincerely,

    Governor

I wrote and mailed this letter on February 11, 2019. I wrote letters to both the Kentucky governor and Louisville mayor.

An Idea for the Teachers' Pension Fund

Dear _____:

I am writing with an idea pertaining to the Teachers' Pension Fund. My idea is to have 5% of revenue accumulated from the Kentucky Lottery and the casino be put into the Teachers' Pension Fund. I am aware that last month, I came up with the idea of using 5% of Kentucky's gambling revenue for furloughed employees, but we can be concerned about furloughed employees if the issue ever again occurs.

Every $1 spent a nickel will go towards the Teachers' Pension Fund. For example, if Kentucky/Louisville makes $100 million in revenue due to the lottery, then $5 million will go into the Teachers' Pension Fund. Also, all winners need to agree to let 5% of their winnings be donated to the Teachers' Pension Fund. The Kentucky Lottery Headquarters is to post a sign on all machines stating that "5% of money going into the machine will be donated to the Teachers' Pension Fund. Also, 5% of what you win will be donated to the Teachers' Pension Fund here in Kentucky/Louisville."

I hope the idea can be discussed and taken into consideration.

Thank you for reading my letter. I deeply appreciate it.

I wrote and mailed this letter on March 16, 2019, to the Kentucky governor.

I kept copies of this letter on my USB drive. I mailed copies to both my state senator and state representative on June 5, 2019.

Getting Rid of Alimony in Kentucky

Dear Governor _____:

I am writing with a concern and an idea. My concern is the number of former spouses who are paying alimony when their former spouse's infidelity was the reason for the divorce. Child support is totally acceptable because it benefits the children, but alimony is unfair to the former paying spouse—especially when the recipient is using the alimony money to benefit their new boyfriend or new girlfriend. For example, a man who is a pharmacist pays more than $1,500 a month to his ex-wife for both child support and alimony. He should be paying child support, but his ex-wife is spending her ex-husband's alimony money on her new man. Child support I am in favor of since it benefits the children. Alimony I am against since it promotes laziness in the former spouse, and the former spouse might use the alimony money on their new boyfriend or girlfriend. Also, the former spouse might have cheated during the marriage.

As we all know, many years ago, a celebrity committed suicide by hanging himself due to his wife threatening to divorce him and taking half of everything. This incident is what motivated me to write this letter.

The ex-wife getting alimony might seem funny in sit-coms such as the doctor who had to move in with his rich brother due to his wife taking half of everything he worked to earn. In real life it is not funny! In real life, it is tragic! Many years ago, I was watching a true crime show and in one episode a young woman wanted to divorce her rich husband and get half of everything. The rich husband hired a hitman to kill her. Although this incident occurred in another state who can day that it cannot occur here in Kentucky?

Let us do away with alimony in Kentucky due to it promoting laziness and too many former spouses are being "rewarded" for their infidelity which is plain wrong! Alimony can also lead to criminal activities such as murder. Please allow the former paying spouses to keep more of the money that they worked to earn. If the recipient ex-wives or ex-husbands need money, then they need to work for it. I work to get money.

I hope you can share this idea with others and that the alimony issue can be discussed.

Thank you for reading my letter. I deeply appreciate it.

*Changes were made from the original letter.

This response letter was written on March 21, 2019. I received it on March 26, 2019.

Dear Ms. Maddox:

Thank you for contacting the Governor's office with your thought about your legislative reforms. I have shared your concerns with the Governor.

In addition, it would be beneficial if you would contact your state legislatures in the General Assembly with your suggestions as any change or addition to the current law would originate in the legislatures.

You may visit: (website address I choose to nor reveal) or call (502) XXX-XXXX to find and contact members of your delegation.

Again, thank you for you writing to the Governor, and we wish you the best in your endeavor.

Sincerely,

Director of Constituent Services

*Some changes were made from the original letter.

This letter was written and mailed on April 1, 2019. I wrote this letter to the mayor of Louisville and a letter to the Kentucky governor.

What Do You Want To Say?

I made copies from my USB drive and mailed letters to both my state senator and state representative on June 5, 2019.

Cool Places to Stay

Dear _____:

I am writing with an idea. Summertime and the hot summer heat will be here before you know it. There are so many people in our city/state who do not have air conditioners in their homes for one reason or another. Some people are on a tight budget and are living from paycheck to paycheck. Many seniors are on a fixed income. Others live in homes with people who have an excellent form of income but are too selfish and/or stingy to install an air conditioner. For example, the homeowner has air conditioners to install but they choose to let every summer be a "no air conditioner" summer. My idea is for our city/state to create more "cool places to stay" during the summertime. I know that libraries are a great place to stay, but we can also allow people to "hang out" at the malls so they can escape their hot homes. I also know of a minister in my neighborhood who would gladly allow me to hang out at his church for a few hours each week. This is a genuine act of compassion. If possible, please encourage more church leaders to open their church fellowship halls during the summer months so that people in their communities can have cool places to stay for a few hours a day.

I hope the idea to create more "cool places" for residents to stay can be discussed and taken into consideration. I also hope that more church leaders can allow members of their communities to stay in their fellowship halls for a few hours a day and an act of compassion. Thank you for reading my letter. I deeply appreciate it.

*I have never received a response about the issue.

I wrote this letter to the Louisville mayor on April 13, 2019.

I made copies to this letter from my USB drive and mailed them to both my senator and representative on May 28, 2019.

An Ideal Location for More Motels

I am writing with an idea. There are many vacant buildings in the Okolona Center, which is located on the corner of Preston Highway and Outer Loop Road. My idea is to turn them into more motels. Many Louisville residents are now living in motels due to financial limitations.

There are many advantages to having motels in the Okolona Center location. Some advantages are as follows:

#1—This location is on the #18 bus line for those who do not have vehicles.

#2—There are an abundance of job opportunities near this area.

#3—There are an abundance of restaurants near this location.

#4—This is driving distance to both a local grocery store and a department store.

#5—There's access to more places than I can name. Restaurants, stores and so on.

I might write a letter to (I added the name, address, and phone to the corporate office of a motel franchise). I hope to see new motels in the Okolona Center soon. I also hope that the issue can be discussed and taken into consideration. Thank you for reading my letter. I deeply appreciate it.

*I have never received a response.

*Changes were made to this letter from the original one.

I wrote and mailed this letter to both the Louisville mayor and the Kentucky governor on May 1, 2019.

Giving Child Support to Custodial Grandparents

Dear Mayor _____:

I am writing with a concern and an idea. My concern is for an elderly widower in my community who is raising granddaughters. The granddaughters' parents are alive and well but choose to "pawn" the responsibility of their children on their paternal grandfather. As my way of helping this elderly widower I have him on my mobile phone plan. Last month, I paid the bill early and it took almost my entire paycheck. I asked for $20 for gas and he did not have it due to the prom expenses of one of his granddaughters. Fortunately for me, my father had the money for gas since my father and I share a car. Although the granddaughters' parents are alive and well, neither of them ever paid him child support. This widower lives on a disability check that he recently started receiving due to his being a wounded Vietnam Vet. His having to raise, feed and support his granddaughters also has a financial effect on both my daughter and me. His late wife and he helped me with my daughter since I am a single mother and my daughter and I are "paying" them back by helping him however possible. The only thing is his granddaughters' parents are taking advantage of him! Both the father and mother of his granddaughters should be required to pay him child support.

My idea is to make it a law for both parents to get jobs and make child support payments to the custodial grandparents (or guardians). If the parents cannot find employment due to a criminal record, then I have an entire list of "Second Chance Employers" that I will be happy to share with them.

If possible, make the child support payments 15% of their paychecks.

Some parents need to stop being comfortable with having babies that others must raise, feed, and financially support. If they are required to pay child support, then (hopefully) they will stop this cycle. I am tired of children being punished for having selfish, negligent, and irresponsible parents. As a preteen and a teenager, I was deprived of basic needs such as deodorant, hair care products, new clothes, new shoes, new underwear and so on. Due to my mother not being in our lives. It hurts me to see other children being deprived of their needs due to their having such irresponsible parents. Please make the parents (both mothers and fathers) pay child support to the custodial grandparents (or guardians)!

I hope the idea of making parents (both mothers and fathers) pay child support to the custodial grandparents (or guardian) can be discussed and taken into consideration.

Thank you for reading my letter. I deeply appreciate it.

*Changes were made to this letter from the original one.

*I never received a response from the Louisville mayor's office.

This letter was written and mailed to me on May 28, 2019, on behalf of the Kentucky governor.

Dear Ms. Maddox:

Thank you for contacting the Office of the Governor. The Governor is committed to providing servant leadership during his administration and recognizes moving the Commonwealth forward requires a team effort. This is to acknowledge receipt of your letter and to let you know that the Governor has asked the Office of the Ombudsman to respond.

I am sorry to hear of the difficulties that you have described and have documented your concerns. The best way to have any law revised is to contact your elected members of the General Assembly.

I have included a brochure that may be helpful to him. He may also contact the Kinship Support Hotline at: 877-XXX-XXXX to see if he could qualify for assistance for his granddaughters.

I hope this has been helpful. If there is anything further, we can assist you with, please do not hesitate to contact my office.

Sincerely,

(Name I choose to not reveal)

Office of the Ombudsman & Administration Review

Cabinet for Health and Family Services

This letter was written and mailed to both the Louisville mayor and Kentucky governor on May 9, 2019.

This same letter was copied from my USB drive and mailed to both my senator and representative on May 28, 2019.

Taxing 5% to Bingo Winners

Dear _____:

I am writing with another idea. There are bingo halls thought Louisville/Kentucky. My idea is to tax a 5% tax to all bingo winners and that 5% goes toward the Teachers' Pension Fund. For example, if a bingo player wins $1,000 then $50 will be deducted from their winnings. All bingo halls should have signs stating that "All winners will have 5% deducted from their winnings and that 5% will go toward 'The Teachers' Pension Fund.'" Hopefully, this would help our state's pension fund be replenished soon.

I hope this idea can be discussed and taken into consideration.

Thank you for reading my letter. I deeply appreciate it.

What Do You Want To Say?

I wrote and mailed this letter to both my senator and representative on May 28, 2019.

Allowing SSI Recipients to Work

Dear _____:

I am writing with a concern and an idea. There are "Now Hiring" signs all around Louisville, but too many people want a job making $13.00/an hour or more. Too many of these jobs start at $8.50 or $9.50 an hour and these positions go unfilled for months. My idea is to allow SSI Recipients to work but give certain limitations. Some of the limitations can include (but, not be limited to) the following:

#1—The SSI Recipient is required to bring a doctor's statement to the job interview to verify what they can or cannot do.

#2—The SSI Recipient must work a job making less than $10.00 an hour. (If they have a job making $9.95 an hour, then it is all right.)

#3—The SSI Recipient cannot work more than 40 hours a week, which means they are not permitted to work overtime. (Preferably 7 hours a day, 5 days a week or 6 hours a day, 6 days a week.)

#4—The employers should be required (by law) to abide by the rules and restrictions of their employees who are SSI Recipients.

I hope these ideas can be discussed and taken into consideration. I know of people who receive SSI for their bad back, but they like to bag up groceries at the grocery stores near their home on a volunteer basis, so they will not have to sit at home and be bored.

Thank you for reading my letter. I deeply appreciate it.

My state senator wrote and mailed a letter on June 5, 2019. I received it a few days later.

Dear Ms. Maddox:

I am in receipt of your letters on how to fund pensions, raise revenue, Supplemental Security Income, and angel trees. Thank you for taking the time to share your views with me. I value hearing from constituents who want to be a part of the civic dialogue.

You raise some good points and have some good ideas on how to help move Kentucky forward. I will keep your ideas in mind as we hold committee meetings during the interim to prepare for the 2020 Regular Session.

Please feel free to contact me anytime that I can be of assistance to you or to express your support or opposition of a bill/issue before the General Assembly.

Sincerely,

State Senator

*A few changes were made to this letter from the original letter.

My state representative wrote and mailed this letter on June 18, 2019. I received it a few days later.

Dear Ms. Maddox:

Thank you so much for offering your opinions on such important issues. I have passed your ideas on to the appropriate committee chairs in these areas. I have been advocating for expanding gaming and using the tax receipts to pay unfunded liabilities in our pensions.

I do like your Angel Tree idea and have forwarded it to the Louisville Salvation Army. You can see the letter I sent to them included with this one.

Thanks again for your ideas, and never hesitate to reach out to me.

Sincerely,

State Representative

*A few changes were made to this letter from the original letter.

My state representative wrote and mailed this letter to the Salvation Army Office in Louisville, Kentucky on June 18, 2019.

To Whom It May Concern:

A constituent of mine named Dorothea Maddox recently wrote to me, and she had some thoughtful recommendations regarding the Angel Tree Program, which I want to relay to you. Dorothea's suggestions mostly had to deal with the color of the angels, which she said should better represent the diversity of the city of Louisville. Instead of just having black or white angels, she would like to see color coded angels, including pink for girls, blue for boys, lavender for infant girls and peach for infant boys. According to Dorothea, these colors would make the angels less centered on race, which make sense the population of Louisville continues to become more and more ethnically mixed.

I hope you will take Dorothea's ideas into consideration at the Salvation Army for the Angel Tree Program. Please do not hesitate to contact me if I can be of further assistance of if you have any questions. Thank you for your assistance in this matter.

Sincerely,

State Representative

This letter was written and mailed to my state representative by the Director of the Salvation Army on July 1, 2019.

Dear _____:

I am writing in response to your letter dated June 18th that shared a concern that constituent Dorothea Maddox shared with you about The Salvation Army Angel Tree Program. Thank you for making us aware and seeking our assistance.

The Angel Tree Program Icons that Dorothea referenced are in fact gender neutral and they have light and darker skin tones—designed to represent *all shades of nationalities.* We do not see our angels as just black or white. The ANGELS truly do represent the diversity of the city of Louisville and the descriptive information that is placed on the Angels is what tells about the child. This information is provided to us by the Parent or Guardian who signs up to get gifts and reflects what they want to be known about "their" angel. This info can include age, nationality, gender identity, sizes, toys and more!

The Salvation Army Angel Tree program is certainly a highlight of our Christmas season and represents 5–6 months of work leading up to the adoption of Angels from the "Trees" to the distribution of gifts to the families. This Christmas program coordination and volunteer management represents our desires that every child wake up Christmas morning to gifts and the joy & surprise of celebrating the special holiday. We know all too well that for families who are living on poverty, the season can for them feel like a burden and add stress with the thought of how to afford gifts when struggling to pay rent or keep the lights on.... BUT the Angel Tree allows the children wake up and know that Mom and Dad, or Grandma.... did not forget them!

We work hard to make sure every Angel is provided as lease two new outfits, a large toy, a small toy, and items from their list. We supplement for Angels when bags are returned and may not contain all the items and we fully provide for forgotten angels when people with good intentions may adopt from the Tree but then they do not return the packages...we understand perhaps something come up for them.

I hope that you and Dorothea will consider volunteering this Christmas at the Joy Center or for the Angel Tree adoption process to see the coordination, logistics, and undertaking it is to provide Christmas for nearly 10,000 area children. It is a labor of love and a source of pride and satisfaction for everyone at The Salvation Army, our volunteers, the families, and our community and corporate partners who step up to help.

Thank you again for sharing and I hope this will enlighten you more to the inclusion of The Salvation Army Angel Tree Program.

Gratefully yours,

Director of Development

I wrote and mailed this letter to a local Pastor in my community on July 29, 2019.

Dear Pastor _____:

I want to thank you for the compassion that you have shown toward the past. I live in a house with no working air conditioner and I sometimes come to the Church for a cool place to stay.

I have not been up to the Church this summer for one reason. I told a Church member the reason why I was coming up to the Church on Tuesdays and Thursdays and his remark was, "You can't get a fan?!" I explained to him that I have a few fans in my house, but my house is still hot. The Church member's remark was, "It sounds to me like you need another fan!" His judgmental comment made me feel so unwelcomed.

I want to explain to you how I got into my present situation:

*I live with my parents and they have no working air conditioner in their house.

*I live with my parents because I lost my house in 2005.

*I lost my house because I lost my financial stability.

*I lost my financial stability due to my working to support myself, my daughter, a young mother and her three small boys.

*The young mother felt as though I owe her a living because my godmother was the grandmother of her first two boys and my godmother did so much for my daughter and me in the past.

*The father of the first two boys felt like I should support his kids for him because of everything his mother did for my daughter and me in the past.

*I had to pay all the bills by myself. Having to support another mother and her children was an obligation beyond my financial means.

*I lost my house and returned to my parents' house.

*I was pressured into enrolling in school. I did not want to enroll in school because I did not want a bunch of school loan debt.

*I finally enrolled in school.

*I now have more than $40,000 in school loans.

*I cannot get my own place to my "mountain" of school loan debt.

*As a result of my not being about to get my own place I must remain in my parents' house.

*My parents have no working air conditioner.

The point of my telling you my story is this: Before anybody makes judgmental comments about others, they must know the other person's situation. It has been said that "behind every situation is a story" and this is my story.

I hope you can understand my situation and please talk to all your congregation members about not making judgmental comments about other people's situations.

Please pray and ask that God restores to me everything that I have lost. I have lost my financial stability, my car, and my house in August of 2005. Please pray and ask that God helps me to pay off all my school loan debt so that I can be self-sufficient. I am 50. I am too old to be living at home with my parents.

Thank you for reading my letter. I deeply appreciate it.

*I called the church a few days after I mailed the letter to find out if the pastor received it. His response was, "You're always welcomed here. This is your house too."

*A church member came to my house and gave me her phone number. We have been friends and helping each other ever since.

*My younger brother, who is a certified HVAC Installer, put central air into our house that following September.

What Do You Want To Say?

I wrote and mailed this letter to a CEO of a major department store on July 29, 2019.

Clothing for Women with Mastectomies

Dear _____:

I am writing with a suggestion. There are many women who have mastectomies due to breast cancer and some of them either cannot afford breast implants or choose to not get them. My suggestion is for (name of store) to come up a selection of clothing for women in these situations—including swimsuits. I know a woman who cannot find an affordable swimsuit for somebody who has had a mastectomy. Many of these women feel like she is "less than a woman" after the surgery. I hope (name of store) can come out with both undergarments and outerwear that make women in these situations still feel like they are women again.

I hope you can come up with a line of clothing for women who have had mastectomies and need prosthetics. Please help women in this situation feel like women again. Thanks in advance.

Thank you for reading my letter. I deeply appreciate it.

This letter was written and mailed on August 13, 2019.

Dear Dorothea,

We have reviewed your letter and want you to know that we have shared it with the appropriate team. We appreciate you taking the time to send us your suggestions.

Your Reference number is: XXXXXX-XXXXXX

Sincerely,

Customer Care

I wrote and mailed this letter on July 31, 2019. I sent copies to the Louisville mayor, the Kentucky governor, my state senator, and my state representative.

Allowing Non-violent Inmates to Work

Dear _____:

I am writing with an idea for eliminating jail over-crowding. My idea is to allow non-violent inmates to be put on work release. The non-violent inmates will include those who are locked up for non-support, bad checks, not paying off cash loans, not paying a driving violation ticket, and so on. I saw a news report in which they are doing this in Hardin County, and this works for them. A van or bus can take the inmates to and from work. The inmates will be able to work all three shifts. There are places in Downtown Louisville and South Louisville who hire those with criminal backgrounds.

The inmates who are put on work-release cannot choose which shifts they work. Instead, their shift will be chosen for them. Also, they cannot choose where to work at. The place will be selected for them.

Those who are assigned to 1st shift will have the following schedule:

Wake up time: 4am

Shower time: 5am

Breakfast: 6am

Work Schedule: 7am to 3pm (or 3:30pm)

Dinnertime: 5pm

Bedtime: 8pm (Sleep time will be 8pm to 4am)

Those who are assigned to 2nd shift will have a daily schedule as follows:

Wake up time: 12pm

Shower time: 1pm

Mealtime: 2pm

Work Schedule: 3pm to 11pm (or 3:30 to midnight)

Mealtime: 1am

Bedtime: 4am (Sleep time will be 4am to 12pm)

Those who are assigned 3rd shift will have the following daily schedule:

Wake up time: 8pm

Shower time: 9pm

Mealtime: 10pm

Work Schedule: 11pm to 7am

Mealtime: 8am

Bedtime: 12pm (Sleep time will be from 12pm to 8pm)

Many factories and warehouses as well as hotels and motels are second-chance employers, but it depends on the offense. Some restaurants are also second-chance employers.

The inmates (or course) will be required to have ankle bracelets on while at work as a way for the jail to keep up with their whereabouts.

To put non-violent inmates on a work schedule will give them work experience. This will also give the inmates an opportunity to pay their child support, their restitution to check-cashing places or other places they owe money to. This will also eliminate jail overcrowding.

I hope this idea can be discussed and taken into consideration.

Thank you for reading my letter. I deeply appreciate it.

*I never received a response.

I wrote and mailed this letter to a drugstore franchise on August 3, 2019.

An Ideal Location for a Drugstore

To Whom It May Concern:

I am writing with an idea. There is a building which sits idle at the corner of Poplar Level Road and East Indian Trail. This location used to be (their rival drugstore). My idea is for your company to turn it into (name of drugstore).

My neighborhood can deeply benefit from having a (name of drugstore) for many reasons. People in my neighborhood can drive a short distance to get their prescription medications. Residents will be able to drive a short distance to buy postage stamps and not have to drive all the way to the post office. This location is on a bus line which means employees will have an easy and convenient way to get to work every day. There are many people in the area who do not have vehicles and they will be able to walk to Walgreens to get whatever they need. There are also many other reasons for why it would be a great idea to put a (name of drugstore) in our neighborhood.

I hope to see a (name of drugstore) in our neighborhood soon.

Thank you for reading my letter. I deeply appreciate it.

*Changes were made to this letter. Name of company I choose to withhold.

This letter was written on August 9, 2019. I received it on August 12, 2019.

Dear Ms. Maddox,

Thank you for your letter regarding an optimal location for our drugstore. I sincerely appreciate when our customers reach out to let us know of ways, we can positively impact the community. We are always looking for ways to grow our brand in a way that is favorable for our customers and our business. We have in fact reviewed that location for a possible drugstore location and while at this time we have passed on this site, you never know what the future holds.

We pride ourselves in supporting and taking care of customers in our communities since 1901. I hope that you will visit our other locations nearby. We look forward to seeing you!

*Some changes were made to this letter.

What Do You Want To Say?

I wrote and mailed this letter to the Louisville mayor, my state senator, and my state representative on August 14, 2019.

Starting a Statewide Ministers' Convention.

Dear _____:

I was watching the news and there was talk about bringing more conventions to Louisville which is a brilliant idea. My idea is to come up with a "Statewide Ministers' Convention" and hold it every other year in Louisville starting 2020. It might be a good idea to have it during the summertime just in case ministers want to bring their children (or grandchildren) along.

The purpose of a Statewide Ministers' Convention is so that ministers throughout Kentucky can build connections with each other. There will be retraining sessions for older (or more seasoned) ministers. The reason for the retraining sessions is so ministers know how to minister to racially diverse congregations. Most churches are no longer all-Black or all-White. There is also an "explosion" of racially mixed people in Louisville, Bardstown, and other places throughout Kentucky. There are people mixed with Black and White; Black and Hispanic; White and Hispanic; Black and Asian; White and Asian; and many other kinds of mixtures. The days of preaching about race-mixing being a sin are over. When the Bible says do not intermarry it was a spiritual issue—not racial. (Deuteronomy 7:2–4; 2 Corinthians 6:14; and 1 Timothy 4:2–4.) As a child, I can remember people telling me that I have sinned by being born since my twin brother and I were born to a White mother and Black father.

There will also be training sessions for new minsters. All ministers have different needs. For example, the needs of ministers at Fort Knox or Fort Campbell are different from the needs of the ministers who have prison ministries. The needs of ministers who preach in rough neighborhoods are different from the need of ministers who have Churches in rural areas. New ministers who preach at Fort Knox or Fort Campbell can "connect" with ministers who preached at military posts for years. New ministers who have prison ministries can "connect" with ministers who preached at prisons for years. New preachers who preach in rough neighborhoods can "connect" with ministers who preached in rough neighborhoods for years. New ministers who preach in rural areas can "connect" with ministers who preached in rural areas for years.

Ideal candidates to preach at the Statewide Minister's Convention can be:

(I gave the names of the most highly known ministers in Louisville, Kentucky).

(I also gave ideal locations for the Statewide Ministers' Conventions).

I hope to see Statewide Ministers' Conventions every other year starting in 2020. Please share this idea with others.

Thank you for reading my letter. I deeply appreciate it.

*I have never received a response to this letter.

*Changes were made to this letter from the original one.

I wrote and mailed this letter to the Kentucky governor, the Louisville mayor, my state senator, and my state representative on August 22, 2019.

Protests near Restaurants

Dear _____:

I am writing with another concern. There are protesters who protest near restaurants. On one occasion, when I was with my daughter and two grandsons, these protesters were across the street from a restaurant on Preston Highway here in Louisville. My daughter then told me a unique story. She was at a restaurant at another location, and she ordered (I believe) a pork chop sandwich. There were protesters near the restaurant, and they began to ridicule my daughter. They said things like, "Do you realize you're eating swine and swine is an unclean animal?!" The only way they knew what she ordered is if they were looking through the restaurant's window. Some restaurants have big windows and people in the street can see inside the restaurant. My daughter and I are Christians who live by Acts 10:13-15 which reads, "Then the voice told him, 'Get up, Peter, Kill and eat.' 'Surely not Lord!' Peter replied. 'I have never eaten anything unclean.' The voice spoke to him a second time, 'Do not call anything impure that God has made clean.'" The point is; if my daughter and I want to eat "swine" then we can. Nobody has the right to ridicule us because of what we eat. I have a niece and a brother who had similar experiences up in Ohio. My brother was approached by a lady who shouted, "Do you realize chickens had to die so you can eat them?!" On another occasion, my niece was leaving a restaurant and a lady who was a vegan approached her and shouted, "Do you realize that baby chickens were deprived of the chance to be born so you can have eggs?!"

My idea is to create a law here in Kentucky which states the protesters are to be more than 100 feet away from restaurants when protesting—especially if food is involved. Vegetarians and vegans cannot ridicule us meat-eaters. People from religious groups cannot ridicule us for choosing to eat "swine."

When I was attending Kentucky State University, I did a paper on the destruction of the Amazon rainforests. There was even a comment about rainforests being destroyed so farmers can have banana plantations, and I decided to boycott bananas at the time. A 55-year-old woman at the table next to mine was eating a banana. I kept my mouth shut, remained at my own table, and left her alone. Although I was a naïve 19-year-old, I had enough wisdom to realize that what she ate was <u>not</u> my business. The point is: what we eat is nobody's else's business.

We are always being encouraged to support local businesses—including restaurants. Protesters holding demonstrations near restaurants and condemning customers because of what they eat can jeopardize a restaurant's business.

I ask that you put yourself in two situations:

First Situation: Imagine yourself being a customer at a restaurant and protesters are watching you through the window to see what you eat. Afterward, when you leave the restaurant, the protesters ridicule you because you ate "swine" with your meal.

Second Situation: You are a restaurant owner and protesters are near your restaurant. These protesters ridicule customers for eating chicken due to chickens having to die so they can be eaten. They even ridicule customers for eating eggs because baby chickens were deprived of the chance to be born so that the customers can have eggs with their meal.

I am aware the constitution allows "Freedom of Speech" and "Freedom of Assembly." But we working-class taxpayers (as well as our children and grandchildren) should be entitled to eat at whatever restaurant we choose without being subject to ridicule.

I was giving my neighbor a ride somewhere and I told him about what happened to my daughter. We later passed a restaurant in our neighborhood which had protesters near the restaurant. My neighbor was on the phone with his girlfriend and telling her about the protesters. He then told her in a joking manner, "you better not let them see you walk out of the restaurant with a rib sandwich because they'll ridicule you for eating 'swine' if they do." The point is: stories like this can spread like wildfire. That is why I think it is a good idea to make it against the law to hold protests near restaurants (especially if food is involved).

I hope that making a law stating that protests are to be more than 100 feet from eating establishments can be considered.

Thank you for reading my letter. I deeply appreciate it.

*Some changes were made from the original letter.

This letter was written and mailed from the Kentucky governor's Office on August 26, 2019. I received the letter on September 4, 2019.

Dear Ms. Maddox:

Thank you for contacting the governor's office with your thought about protests near restaurants. I have shared your concerns with the Governor.

It would be beneficial if you would contact your state legislators in the General Assembly with your suggestions as any change or addition to the current law must originate in the state legislature.

You may visit: (website address I choose to not reveal) or call (502) XXX-XXXX to find and contact members of your delegation.

Again, thank you for writing to the governor. Please do not hesitate to contact my Office of Constituent Services in the future on any matter of importance to you. 502-XXX-XXXX.

Sincerely,

Director of Constituent Services

I wrote and mailed this letter to the Louisville mayor as well as my state senator, and my state representative on September 7, 2019.

Keeping Angel Tree Recipients Safe

Dear _____:

I am writing with a serious concern. My concern is keeping all Angel Tree Recipients safe when they go to apply for Angel Tree as well as when they go to receive their gifts.

Many years ago, I received terroristic threats from another client. Although my only child is 26, she was 15 at the time which means this incident occurred almost 11 years ago. But I have relatives, neighbors and friends who will be Angel Tree Recipients soon and I want them to be safe from terroristic threats and unfair situations. Here is how the incident started: A young mother cut to the front of the line. A group of us tried to scream out to the volunteers about how she cut line, but the volunteers ignored us. Another mother looked at me and shouted, "Snitches end up in stitches and in the hospital!" At first, I did not realize she was talking to me. The other mother, again, looked at me and shouted, "Bitches who are snitches end up in stitches and in the hospital!" She then looked at me and said, "I stab bitches who are snitches and I put them in the hospital!" I then stood in line terrified. After the young mother who cut line signed up, she stood next to the mother who threatened me and said, "I will be getting driver's plate numbers, I will be finding our addresses and you will end up in a body bag!" Since she was standing next to the mother who threatened to stab me and put me in the hospital, I stayed quiet and said nothing. I am glad this was the last year for me to do Angel Tree.

My idea is to create a list of rules for recipients to follow and encourage people to volunteer as security guards to be sure all recipients abide by the rules.

Starting this year there should be set rules for all recipients to follow. Ideal rules can be:

1. Do not cut line. Wait your turn like everybody else.
2. No pushing other out of line so that you can be next.
3. Neither verbal abuse nor terroristic threats will be tolerated.
4. Physical violence of any kind will not be tolerated.
5. If you break the rules the first time, then you will be sent to the end of the line.
6. If you break the rules a second time, then you will be sent home and you must come back the next business day.
7. If you break the rules a third time, then you will be sent home and you must come back next week.

8. If you break the rules a fourth time, then you will not be able to sign up this year.

9. If you break the rules a fifth time, then you will never be able to sign up for Angel Tree in Louisville, Kentucky, again.

You can encourage undercover police officers to volunteer as security guards. Another idea is to encourage bouncers from local bars and clubs to be volunteers. You can also encourage martial arts instructors to be volunteers. Of course, all recipients are to be warned that Undercover police officers, bouncers and martial arts Instructors are volunteering as security guards. This will get all recipients to abide by the rules. I hope these ideas can be discussed and considered. Thank you for reading my letter. I deeply appreciate it.

*I never received a response to this letter.

I wrote and mailed this letter to the Louisville mayor as well as my state senator, and my state representative on September 10, 2019.

Have the Casino Work with the Child Support Division.

Dear _____:

I am writing with another idea. My idea is to have casino work with the Child Support Office.

#1—If a person wins over $1,000 then they are to get a ticket.

#2—They are to take the ticket up to the desk.

#3—The desk attendant will view the winner's ID (Driver's license, military ID and so on).

#4—The winner's names and date of birth will be put into the computer.

#5—If the winner owes child support, then a "red flag" will show.

#6—The casino will have a portion of the winnings transferred over to the Child Support Office.

#7—Depending on the financial obligation, the winner either gets whatever is left over or walks away empty-handed.

Just like the Kentucky lottery is required to cooperate with the Child Support System, the casino should also be required to cooperate with the Child Support System. It is not right to allow helpless children to be deprived of their needs while parents splurge at the casino. If the parents owe child support, then they should be required to give a portion (or all) of their winnings to the custodial parents or guardians.

I hope the idea of having the casino corporate with the Child Support System can be discussed and taken into consideration.

Thank you for reading my letter. I deeply appreciate it.

*I never received a response from this letter.

What Do You Want To Say?

I wrote and mailed this letter to the Louisville mayor as well as my state senator, and my state representative. I believe I wrote and mailed this letter on September 12, 2019.

Police Checking Public Parks at Dusk

Dear _____:

I am writing with another concern and an idea. A few months ago, my daughter held a birthday party for my youngest grandson in a local park. Relatives and friends also came. All of us noticed three children who were not being attended to. The boy appeared to be 8; his first sister appeared to be 6; and his second sister appeared to be 4. The boy was bullying some of the other children. My daughter went to the other side of the park to tell his mother. But the mother was surrounded many men and was too busy enjoying their company. The oldest girl got sick and vomited in the sprinkler. All of us attended to her.

When my daughter took the little girl to the other side of the park to explain to their mother what happened, she behaved like she did not care. Again, she was too busy enjoying all the male attention she was receiving. My daughter brought her back around and the oldest girl went back to playing. The youngest girl wanted to attend the party and we allowed her to do so.

At dusk, all of us were exhausted from the birthday party. We were cleaning up and preparing to leave. My oldest grandson left with my friend so that he can stay the night with her two grandsons. My youngest grandson left with his mother and me. My niece had her infant son with her. The point is: all our children and grandchildren were accounted for. Later that night, I was taking a shower and the children in the park suddenly popped in my mind. Since it was 10:00 at night, I was hoping that they were not left in the park.

My idea is to have Police Officers check the public parks at dusk to be sure no children are left unattended or just left in the park by themselves. Just like everywhere else, Louisville does have kidnappers and human traffickers "trolling" parks and other areas with crowds of people. Defenseless children who are left unattended are an incredibly easy target for kidnappers and human traffickers. I am aware that children being kidnapped and exploited has occurred for centuries but let us do what we can to prevent is as much as possible here in Louisville.

I hope the idea of having police officers check public parks at dusk for unattended children can be discussed and taken into consideration.

Thank you for reading my letter. I deeply appreciate it.

*I never received a response from this letter.

What Do You Want To Say?

I wrote and mailed this letter to the Louisville mayor, my state senator, and my state representative on September 21, 2019.

Turning XXXX Poplar Level Road to a Truck Stop

Dear _____:

I am writing with another idea. How about turning a former department store location at: XXXX Poplar Level Road to a Truck Stop for semi-trucks? There are many stories about accidents occurring with semis due to the drivers driving while sleep deprived. My idea is to allow the XXXX Poplar Level Road location to be a Stop-and-Sleep place for semi-truck drivers. The former department store can be turned to men's bathrooms and shower rooms as well as ladies' bathrooms and shower rooms.

There are many advantages to the XXXX Poplar Level Road location being available to semi-truck drivers. Some advantages are:

#1—It is off Watterson Expressway (a major highway here in Kentucky).

#2—It is next to a restaurant.

#3—It is next to a major grocery store.

#4—This prevents Truckers from coming through Louisville and causing major accidents due to their driving while sleep deprived.

Many Truckers and their passengers have sleeping areas in their trucks already. This location will be an excellent place to just stop for a few hours of sleep while going from point A to point B. I do not know if the location is big enough, but I hope it is.

Making XXXX Poplar Level Road a truck stop so that tuckers can stop, and sleep can <u>prevent</u> semi accidents in Louisville due to truckers driving while sleep deprived. This specific area is also next to Watterson Expressway, near a restaurant and a major grocery store.

I hope this idea can be discussed and taken into consideration.

Thank you for reading my letter. I deeply appreciate it.

Sincerely,

P.S. This location can <u>also</u> be used for those traveling in R.V.s and regular vehicles.

*I never received a response from this letter.

What Do You Want To Say?

I wrote and mailed this letter to the Administrative Offices of the Jefferson County Public School system in early October of 2019.

Prospective Career Paths for High School Seniors

Dear _____:

I am writing with an idea. My idea is to encourage some high school seniors in investigate apprenticeship programs instead of college since the cost of college it so high. Some apprenticeship programs to investigate are:

(I gave information to three places that can be investigated).

You can also encourage high school seniors to consider joining the Kentucky National Guard or the United States military (any branch). Many students come from family of extreme financial limitations. For example, some students live in single-parent homes; some students live with grandparents who are on fixed incomes; some students live with older siblings; some students live with an aunt and uncle who really cannot afford to support them, but they do not want to see the student go into a group home. I first moved to Louisville in 1985 when I was 16. I lived with an aunt who could not afford to support me. To make matters worse, I had a hard time getting a job. I could not live with my father due to circumstances beyond my control. Also, my birthmother could not take my twin brother and me because we would interfere with her marriage. Her third husband never knew my twin brother and I existed and her taking us in would have destroyed her marriage. My brother ended up in Bloomfield, Kentucky, with our paternal grandparents and I ended up here in Louisville with an aunt.

You can even encourage students to join the Job Corps after high school. Nobody told me about Job Corps while I was in high school and I wish that somebody would have. It is free job training as well free dorm rooms and free meals while on campus. In other words, Job Corps is a "free college." During my senior year in high school college recruiters came to our school and persuaded us to attend a traditional four-year college. My problem was: nobody in my family had the money to pay for college and financial aid was barely enough to cover books. I also never qualified for scholarship money due to my 2.0 grade point average. To make matters worse, my maternal grandparents were <u>not</u> allowed to pay for my brother's and my education because my mother's third husband might have found out we exist, and it could have destroyed her marriage. I was going to enlist in the Army, but it worried my aunt since I was an attractive young lady at 18 and she felt as though men would use me for bad purposes if I enlisted in the military. In fact, my entire family felt this way. The same night I graduated from high school, I celebrated my graduation at other relatives' house because my aunt's husband put me out of his house. The day after I graduated, my aunt had my things packed up and told me I was going to live with another aunt in Radcliff. This aunt also could not afford to have me there and jobs are extremely scarce. If high school counselors were to inform me of the Job Corps Program, then I would have enlisted right out of high school. I might have been a Nationally Certified Pharmacy Technician. Hospitals throughout Louisville and other parts of Kentucky are in desperate need of Nationally Certified Pharmacy Technicians. The Job Corps Programs provide this kind of training among other kinds of training for free.

If possible, high school counselors should get to know students' situations. I will use this fictional scenario as an example: There is a young lady named Carmelita who was relocated to Louisville from Puerto Rico after Hurricane Maria hit her island. She lives with an uncle who is a widower and gets a monthly widows' check. She works at a local restaurant to be able to afford to buy herself the basics such as hair care products, deodorant, underwear, socks, feminine products, school supplies, and so on. Carmelita and her family have no way of paying for college! This is an example of why it is ignorant for college recruiters to come into schools and say things like, "You should go to college to pursue a degree and your parents should pay for it." These college recruiters do not know the situations of each of these high school students!

Many high school seniors come from families with financial limitations, and they should be introduced to other ways of pursuing great-paying careers without it having to be a four-year traditional college. Students can be encouraged to join an apprenticeship program or the Kentucky National Guard as a way of paying for college or the United States military (any branch) or the Job Corps Program.

I hope these ideas can be discussed and taken into consideration.

Thank you for reading my letter. I deeply appreciate it.

I received this letter from the Administrative Offices of the Jefferson County Public School System on October 16, 2019.

Dear Dorothea Maddox:

Thank you so much for sharing your story with us. It is a powerful testament of your resilience and highlights an area of growth for JCPS. We recognize that we were leaving many of our students out of opportunities by having such a strong focus on college going. We recognize that many of our students do not fit into a tradition, four-year college going mold and should have other options presented to them. Over the past few years, we have been making the shift to provide access to the types of learning opportunities you describe in your letter.

In 2016–17 we started an initiative in 11 of our high schools that focused on opening access for ALL students to Career and Technical Education. The Academics of Louisville initiative brings local business to the table to partner with our high schools to expand learning opportunities including internships and other work-based learning. Through the Academics of Louisville, we can help students get credentials before leaving high school leading to a pathway directly to the workforce if that is the student's choice.

We believe in the pipeline to work so much and opportunities that an apprenticeship could provide to our students that JCPS had signed on to be a registered apprenticeship with the state of Kentucky. We even sought and were awarded a grant to help expand apprenticeship opportunities in our community. You are so right about our young people needing to learn and grow AND work!

We will also continue to help grow our school counselors and provide opportunities for them to learn about options for students. Job Corps, military, UPS Metropolitan College, UPS Earn to Learn, Work Ready Kentucky Scholarship,

Kentucky Fame, and Build Kentucky are just a few of the options available for students who want to get certified or an associate degree—many of which have built in work opportunities and or tuition reimbursement. We will be hosting a school day college and career fair where students can learn about ALL these opportunities including our partners offering apprenticeships and summer working opportunities.

Your letter reminds us that we still have a lot of work ahead of us to ensure that ALL students know their options and can chart their paths to achieve their goals. I do not know if you were able to achieve your dreams of becoming a Pharmacy Technician. If so, congratulations. If not and you are still interested, I would encourage you to reach out to the Kentucky Health Career Center. They may be able to connect you to training opportunities and employment in

Healthcare. They can be reached at: 502-XXX-XXXX (Ask for KHCC) or at their center at: XXX XXXXX Street.

Sincerely,

Assistant Superintendent of High Schools

Academic School Division.

*Some names, phone numbers and locations I choose to not reveal.

I wrote and mailed this letter to a property manager, a public housing office, and the Louisville mayor as well as my state senator and my state representative on October 19, 2019.

Unsupervised Children Playing in the Street

To Whom It May Concern:

I am writing about a major concern. On Saturday, October 19th, I was driving down the road and I was at a stop sign, about to turn right. I looked to my left and saw three children playing in the street. I honked my horn at them and a boy who was lying in the middle of the street quickly got up. I then rolled down my window and yelled, "Get out of the street!" The two boys quickly got out of the street, but the one girl put her hand on her hip and gave me a "who are you?" look. I then shouted, "Get out of the street now!" The girl quickly got out of the street. I do not know whose children they were, but it concerns me that some parents (or guardians) are not watching these children. If these children were to get hit by vehicles, then the parents (or guardians) will be looking for somebody to hold accountable.

Please talk to all parents (and guardians) about watching these children and keeping them safe. Please let them know they are accountable for whatever happens to their children. If possible, please post signs in all apartment complexes stating that children war always to be watched and supervised. The sign can say something like:

Parents (and guardians):

You are always to watch your children. If anything happens to them, then you are accountable. Thank you for your cooperation.

I hope that the situation can be addressed and taken care of.

Thank you for reading my letter. I deeply appreciate it.

*Some changes were made to this letter.

*I never received any response pertaining to this letter.

What Do You Want To Say?

I wrote and mailed this letter to the Louisville mayor, my state senator, and my state representative on October 24, 2019.

Having Strip Clubs Cooperate with the Child Support Division

Dear _____:

I am writing with another idea. My idea is to have "gentlemen clubs" and other adult establishments cooperate with the Child Support Division. The owners will hang up photos of those who are delinquent on their child support payments, but the photos will be out of sight of the customers. Also, the establishment will only have photos of those who live in the zip code of the establishment.

Fictional Scenario:

A strip club called "Sweethearts" is in the 40128 zip code. The photos of delinquents who live in the 40218 zip code will be posted in areas out of sight of the customers. When customers enter the building, a person sits at a podium and checks their IDs. The photos can be posted inside the podium and out of the sight of the customers. If a person whose delinquent in their child support payments enters then they can be allowed to enter. After the person enters, the owner is to call a police officer from the closest police division. The delinquent person will be escorted to a back area, arrested, and taken out through a back door.

I am not trying to take away business from any establishments. But it is so unfair for helpless children to continue to be deprived of what they need while their deadbeat parents (both fathers and mothers) "make it rain" at strip clubs every Saturday night. Also, last year, a struggling mother posted a photo on social media which shows a long line of mothers who were there to sign their children up for Salvation Army Angel Tree gifts. In the next photo, there were fathers who were "making it rain" at a strip club. All I ask is that all adult entertainment establishments be required to corporate with the child support division.

I hope to make it a requirement for Adult Entertainment Establishments cooperate with the Child Support Division can be discussed and taken into consideration.

Thank you for reading my letter. I deeply appreciate it.

*I never received any response pertaining to this letter.

What Do You Want To Say?

I wrote and mailed this letter to the Louisville mayor, my state senator, and my state representative on November 2, 2019.

Transparency on the Ballots

Dear _____:

I am writing with another idea. Staring in 2020, have ballots indicate whether a candidate is Pro-Life or Pro-Choice. Not all Democrats are pro-choice and not all Republicans are pro-life. Also, Independents can be either pro-life or pro-choice. On the ballots, "PC" will mean pro-choice, and "PL" will mean pro-life.

The ballot can look like this:

Kentucky governor:

John Doe (D) (PC)

Jack Spratt (R) (PL)

Jill Hill (I) (PC)

Louisville mayor:

Sylvester Fox (D) (PC)

Shannon Choi (R) (PL)

Julie Jones (I) (PC)

Every Election Year many Christians put signs in their yards which read, "Vote Life" but when I go to the polls to vote, I am not sure which ones on the ballots are pro-choice or pro-life. Just like many Catholics and other Christians are always voting for the candidates who are pro-life, there are many liberals who are pro-choice. All of us have the right to know which candidates are pro-life and which candidates are pro-choice. Many voters have extremely busy lives, and we do not have the time to pay attention to all campaign commercials. Some voters work 10-hour or 12-hour shifts and when they get home, they're too exhausted to pay attention to which candidates are what. Some voters even have parents, grandparents, or great-grandparents to look after. But, when we go to vote, we have the right to have some transparency when it comes to serious issues such as abortion. For many voters, abortion is one of the top issues.

I hope that indicating whether a candidate is pro-life or pro-choice on the ballots can be discussed and considered.

Thank you for reading my letter. I deeply appreciate it.

*I never received a response pertaining to this letter.

What Do You Want To Say?

I wrote and mailed this letter to the Louisville mayor on November 22, 2019.

Louisville's Surplus Rainy-Day Fund

Dear _____:

I am writing with another idea. I was watching the 4:00 news this past Friday and it was brought to my attention that Louisville has a surplus Rainy-Day Fund. If possible, I hope that money can be invested in two footbridges here in Louisville. The first footbridge can be placed over the busiest part of Dixie Highway. The second footbridge would go over Bardstown Road at Goldsmith Lane. To have footbridges on both Dixie Highway and Bardstown Road can eliminate both casualties and injuries.

I hope the surplus money can be used to build two footbridges here in Louisville. This can save many, many lives in the future.

Thank you for reading my letter. I deeply appreciate it.

This response letter was written and mailed on December 13, 2019.

Dear Dorothea,

I would like to thank you very much for your continued correspondence and ideas. Your love for our city and interest in seeing it improve for all its residents is obvious and commendable.

At their December 12 meeting, Metro Council chose to invest out surplus in the way that I had proposed. We moved a recruit class up one month while also investing in future pension payments and our rainy-day fund. Increasing pension costs from the state are causing a strain to our city budget which, along with Metro Council's choice not to raise revenue, forced us to make may cuts to city department across the board, including our public safety officials. I believe the choices we made with this surplus were a fiscally responsible thing to do.

Thank you again for sending me letters! Have a happy holiday season!

Sincerely,

(Name I choose to withhold)

Mayor

What Do You Want To Say?

I wrote and mailed this letter the person who was head of the Kentucky Agriculture Department and the Kentucky governor on January 31, 2020.

The Grain Farms in Meade County

Dear _____:

I am writing with an idea. I have been watching the news pertaining to the grain farms in Meade County. My idea it to help the farmers relocate to Nelson County if possible. Some prospective areas are Bloomfield, Fairfield, Cox's Creek, New Haven, Lebanon Junction, Vine Grove, and Wakefield. I have lived in Bloomfield for a year when I was a teenager, and it was a great experience for me. The town is filled with great people.

If possible, I hope the grain bins and grain farmers can be relocated to Nelson County.

Thank you for reading my letter. I deeply appreciate it.

*I received an email response from the Head of the Kentucky Agriculture Department, and they were saying that Nelson County does not have the water source the grain farmers need.

This response letter was written and mailed on February 10, 2020. I received this response letter from the Kentucky governor on February 12, 2020.

Dear Ms. Maddox:

Thank you for taking the time to contact me regarding grain farmers in Nelson County. I appreciate your thoughts and views on issues facing the Commonwealth. As your newly elected Governor, I intend to lead by example, and I will strive to build an administration that does the same. I am committed to the idea and an ideal that we will come together for the common good of all people.

We are all on the same team—**Team Kentucky**, and I am grateful for your willingness to be involved in Kentucky's future.

It is an honor to serve as your Governor and I look forward to your continued feedback. Please contact me in the future on any matter of importance to you.

Sincerely,

(Hand-written signature)

Governor

What Do You Want To Say?

I wrote and mailed this letter to the Louisville mayor, my state senator, and my state representative on February 24, 2020.

Car Seats and Booster Seats

Dear _____:

I am writing with another concern. I am aware the law requires for children to be in car seats and/or booster seats until he or she is 8. I have a grandson who recently turned 7 and is taller than most boys his age. When he gets into a booster seat his head almost touches the ceiling. My idea is to also allow the child's height and weight determine whether a child should be required to be in a booster seat. Some children are taller than most children their age. Some children are larger than most children their age. I hope the booster seat laws can take some of these circumstances into consideration. My oldest grandson's father is (I believe) 6 feet tall.

I do not want to break the law by not having my 7-year-old grandson in a booster. On the other hand, I do not want his riding experience to be a painful one.

I hope height and weight can be considered when it comes to the "booster seat" law.

Thank you for reading my letter.

*I only received a letter from my state representative.

I received this letter from my state representative on March 12, 2020.

Dear Ms. Maddox:

Thank you for taking the time to write me regarding your thoughts on various issues important to you. I am sympathetic to your grandson's issues with using a booster seat, however, we may no longer need one depending upon his height. I have enclosed the statute on car seat and booster seat usage. Your views are always extremely important to me and help me to better serve you, my constituent.

I have started providing periodic updates via email to my constituents while we are in session. Please forward an email address to me if you would like to receive these updates. I can be reached at: XX.XXXXXX@lrc.ky.gov.

Again, thank you for your thoughts on this matter.

Sincerely,

(Hand-written signature)

State Representative

What Do You Want To Say?

I wrote and mailed this letter to some libraries near my home on February 24, 2020.

Flash Drives

To Whom It May Concern:

I am writing with an idea. I know some people leave their flash drives in the computers. My idea is to give people 30 days to claim their flash drives. If they are not claimed within 30 days, then sell the flash drives for $5 each. Of course, the money will be used to benefit the library. This idea is a great advantage to avid writers like me. To pay $5 for a flash drive at the library is better than buying them for $25 or $30 at a local store.

I hope the idea of selling abandoned flash drives for $5 each can be discussed and considered.

Thank you for reading my letter.

*I never received a response from this letter.

What Do You Want To Say?

I wrote and mailed this letter to the Louisville mayor on February 24, 2020.

Too Many Logistics Buildings

Dear _____:

I am writing with another concern and other ideas. My concern of the buildings being built and not being occupied.

An example is the vacant building on the corner of Fern Valley Road and Jefferson Boulevard. That building has been unoccupied for months (maybe over a year). There is another building being built on Shepherdsville Road near Fern Valley Road and Whispering Hills. All I ask is that no more buildings to be built until after all the already built logistics buildings are occupied.

A major concern pertaining to the overdevelopment around Louisville is that deer run into the street because they have nowhere to go. I have coworkers who drive to Louisville from Spencer County, Bullitt County, Nelson County, and other counties. They had near collisions with deer. This is dangerous for both the driver and the deer. I wish all the deer can be relocated to Spencer County, Nelson County, Washington County and Bullitt County. I do not know if that is ever possible. To make matters worse, birds are dying due to their homes being cut down so that more buildings can go up.

Until all the vacant logistics buildings are occupied, it might not be a good idea to build more logistics buildings. Another idea is to tear down abandoned buildings and put up new buildings in the place of the old buildings instead of always tearing up virgin land.

I hope the idea of no more logistics buildings being built until after all the other vacant buildings are occupied can be discussed and taken into consideration.

Thank you for reading my letter. I deeply appreciate it.

*I never received a response from this letter.

I wrote and mailed this letter to the Kentucky governor on February 24, 2020.

Thank you Letter to the Kentucky Governor

Dear Governor _____:

I want to say, "Thank you." Thank you for allowing the Passport Center in West Louisville to finish being built. Many people in Louisville are in desperate need of passport assistance—especially small children and senior citizens. Receiving Passport (Medicaid) does not lead to laziness like some other politicians believe. Instead, the Passport Program helps parents with financial struggles as well as senior citizens and those taking care of disabled children and/or adult relatives.

The Passport Center will also bring job creativity. I wish we can have other Passport Centers throughout Louisville. But I do not know if it is possible.

Thank you for reading my letter. I deeply appreciate it.

P.S. If other Passport Centers can be established in Louisville, then there are vacant buildings in South Central Louisville.

*I never received a response letter.

I wrote and mailed this letter to the CEO of a National Dollar Store Franchise on (I believe) February 5, 2020.

An Idea for a Dollar Store

Dear _____:

I am writing with an idea. Your store is a great place to shop, and your company has great clearance sales. My idea is to have 50%, 70% and 90% off sales on prior season items.

<u>Ideal Examples:</u>

March 1st to May 31st

Spring items=100% retail

Winter items=50% off

Fall items=70% off

Last summer items=90% off

June 1st to August 31st

Summer items=100% retail

Spring items=50% off

Winter items=70% off

Prior fall items=90% off

This idea can also be done with school clothes and school supplies.

Ideal Example:

June 1st to August 31st

School clothes and supplies=100% retail

September 1st to November 30th

School clothes and supplies=50% off

December 1st to February 28th

School clothes and supplies=70% off

March 1st to May 31st

School clothes and supplies=90% off

There are many adults who are raising grandchildren, great-grandchildren, nephews, nieces, cousins, and younger siblings as well as their own children. To have grandparents raising their grandchildren has become a "norm." When I was working at a children's department store many years ago, I witnessed a couple buy their infant granddaughter a snowsuit in August only because it was 70% off. For example, if the original price was $50, then they bought it for only $15. This couple did what they could for their granddaughter. The clearance sales can also be used for seasonal items. For example, after December 26th sell all Christmas items for 90% off to make space for the Valentine's Day items. I will gladly buy a $10 box of Christmas cards for only $1 and use the Christmas cards next year. I hope the idea of 50%, 70% and 90% off clearance off sales can be discussed and considered. Thank you for reading my letter. I deeply appreciate it.

*I received a positive response letter as well as a $25 gift card for my idea. I received this response letter on February 21, 2020.

Dear Ms. Maddox:

My name is _____ and I am the Chief Merchandiser Officer for the store corporation. Our CEO, _____, forwarded me your letter and I wanted to reply personally to your ideas. My first reaction was "Wow!"; thank you so much for the thoughtfulness of your letter, engagement, and connection to our store. At our Corporate Office, we always talk about ensuing the Customer is at the center of everything we do, and your correspondence only emphasized how important that is.

Here are some of my thoughts around Clearance Events:

- We discount seasonal clothing and seasonal stationery every year after the season; we want our customers to get a great value without having to wait until next year.
- We also run nine (9) separate Clearance Events throughout the year in which customers can take advantage of an additional 50%–70% already discounted products.

That said, I have forwarded your commentary to our Pricing Director and we will be discussing how we can indeed even drive more value for the Customers that need it thru our Clearance Events. Again, I appreciate your passion and sharing your ideas with us. Please accept this $25 gift card as a small token of my gratitude and for your continued patronage of our store.

Sincerely,

(Name I choose to withhold)

EVP, Chief Merchandising Officer

What Do You Want To Say?

I wrote and mailed this letter to the Louisville mayor on February 27, 2020.

Beware of Dog Signs

Dear _____:

I am writing with another idea. It was brought to my attention that one man sued another man because the other man's dog bit him. The other man posted a "Beware of Dog" sign on his property, but the other man cannot read. The first man's inability to read is why he was able to sue the dog owner.

My idea is to produce signs which show a dog with big teeth. The sign can also show a stick person being bitten by the dog. The sign will be understood by those who cannot read as well as those who do not know English.

In 2001, my twin brother visited Australia for two weeks. Many lakes have alligators in them. Around the lakes are signs that show a stick person being eaten by an alligator. This sign can be understood by those who cannot read as well as those who speak other languages. I hope this idea can be used for a "Beware of Dog" sign.

Thank you for reading my letter.

*I never received a response letter.

I wrote and mailed this letter to the Louisville mayor on March 11, 2020.

Busing

Dear _____:

I am writing with another idea. I was watching the News and they were talking about budget cuts in the Jefferson County Public School System. The "cutbacks" included busing. My idea is to have all school-aged children attend the schools close to their homes. For example, do not bus the children from Downtown to Jeffersontown. Instead, all the children who live in Downtown attend schools close to their homes. Also, do not bus children from Okolona to West Louisville. Instead, all the children in Okolona should attend schools close to their homes. I believe this would save "boat loads" of money spent on gas to fuel the buses.

I am aware that Louisville is trying to bring racial balance to all the public schools. From what I see, our neighborhoods are becoming more racially diverse. When I moved to Louisville in 1985, at age 16, my neighborhood was predominantly Black. My neighborhood now has a growing number of Whites, Hispanics, Asian-Americans, and Arabs. Many years ago, I knocked on a door to ask about a toy at the curb in front of the house. The homeowner was an Italian man with a thick New York accent. This is an example of our neighborhood growing more racially diverse. If possible, have all students in Public Schools attend the schools closest to their homes.

Some advantages to students attending school closest to their homes are:

#1—More students will be able to walk home instead of spending hours on a bus.

#2—Some parents cannot drive. If an emergency occurs with their child, then the parents who cannot drive will be able to get to their children more quickly.

#3—The bus drivers will not be using so much gas due to busing students from one end of Louisville to the other.

Many years ago, I was at a 25-year class reunion and a woman I attended high school with told me a unique story. She was telling me about the "busing" in 1974. The Jefferson County Public School System was going to bus her all the way to a school in the Shawnee Area of West Louisville when her family and she live in the Okolona Area. Her mother was a diabetic and unable to drive due to her medical condition. If an emergency occurred, then her mother would have no way to pick her up from school. Her parents put her into a Catholic School near their home.

I hope the concerns and ideas in this letter can be discussed and shared with others.

Thank you for reading my letter. I deeply appreciate it.

*I never received a response.

I wrote and mailed this letter to the Louisville mayor, my state senator, and my state representative on March 30, 2020.

Court-Ordered Child Support

Dear _____:

It was recently brought to my attention that many Americans will receive a stimulus check soon. If a person who owes court-ordered child support also receives a stimulus check, then their check should go to the child support division and divided among the custodial parents (or guardian). Regardless of the circumstances throughout the world, children will always be in need. Children will always need food in their stomachs, clothes on their backs, shoes on their feet, a roof over their heads, and so on. The absent parent should be required to fulfill his or her financial obligation regardless of the circumstances around us.

If parents who are not paying his or her court-ordered child support do receive a stimulus check, then it should be taken from them and distributed among the custodial parents or guardians. I hope it is possible to do this.

Thank you for reading my letter. I deeply appreciate it.

*I do not remember if I received a response.

I wrote and mailed this letter to the Louisville mayor on March 30, 2020.

Military People with Work Experience

Dear _____:

I am writing with another idea. There are military (or ex-military) people living in Louisville due to being assigned to Fort Knox. Many of them have tons of work experience, but no papers to prove it. For example, I met a man who has tons of auto mechanic experience, but no papers to prove it. My idea is to encourage places of employment to make these qualified jobseekers take tests to prove that he or she qualifies for the job. We have many auto shops that are in desperate need of experienced and certified mechanics. We also have military (or ex-military) people with tons of experience, but no papers to prove it. The auto shop owners should allow these jobseekers to do a series to tests to prove that he or she is qualified for the job. Of course, the jobseekers will be required to present a resume. The employer will be required to call or email all trainers and past employees.

Many military and ex-military people move to Louisville due to being assigned to Fort Knox. Many of them have tons of work experience, but no papers to prove it. My idea is to encourage employers to give them a series of tests to prove they qualify for the jobs they are pursuing.

Many hospitals in Louisville are in desperate need of Nationally Certified Pharmacy Technicians. If a military or ex-military person applies for a pharmacy technician job at a hospital, then he or she should be able to take the test at the employers' expense. If they pass, then they get the job.

I hope for military and ex-military people with work experience and no papers to prove it can be allowed to take a test (or tests) to get the career they are trying to pursue.

Thank you for reading my letter. I deeply appreciate it.

*I do not remember receiving a response letter.

What Do You Want To Say?

I wrote and mailed this letter to the Louisville mayor on April 18, 2020.

Clothing Stores

Dear Mayor _____:

I am writing with another idea. Many clothing stores are shut down due to their not being an "essential" business. My idea is to allow local clothing and shoe stores to post their items on face book (or online). The customers can call the store to ask if something is still available. If the item is available, then the customer can give their credit (or debit) card information to the Store Manager over the phone. If the card successfully goes through, then the customer can pick up their items by "curb pick-up."

Example:

#1—I go online and discover they have some maxi dresses for sale.

#2—I call the store to ask if they still have the items.

#3—The store manager says, "yes."

#4—I give the store manager my card information.

#5—My card information successfully goes through.

#6—The store manager allows me to pick up my items at 2pm by "curb pick-up."

We do this for restaurants to help their employers stay employed. I hope we can do this for employers at clothing and shoe stores too.

I hope our country opens back up soon. I also hope this pandemic ends soon. Just in case it does not, I hope clothing and shoe stores can also be considered as "essential."

Thank you for reading my letter. I deeply appreciate it.

*I never received a response letter.

I wrote and mailed this letter to the CEO of a Dollar Store Franchise on April 22, 2020.

Vacant Property

Dear _____:

I am writing with an idea. I have an idea for a store which is located at: XXXX Poplar Level Road here in Louisville, Kentucky. There used to be a furniture store next door, but now it is empty. My idea is for your company to buy the empty area and expand the store, if possible. To have a bigger store will have some advantages:

Some of the advantages are:

#1—More space for merchandise.

#2—Have a side for items being sold for retail and a side for clearance items.

#3—Have clutter-free aisles.

Your store is a great place to shop. But sometimes some of the isles have too much "stuff." To alleviate space, your company can buy the empty space next door, tear down the wall and make the store bigger.

I hope your company can buy the empty space next to: XXXX Poplar Level Road in Louisville, Kentucky. I hope this location can be expanded.

Thank you for reading my letter. I deeply appreciate it.

*I never received a response letter.

I wrote and mailed this letter on the Louisville mayor, my state senator, and my state representative on May 13, 2020.

Studio Apartments

Dear _____:

I am writing with another idea. There are many people who are homeless or living in an overcrowded house due to rent being so high. My idea is to encourage property managers to buy abandoned houses as well as other buildings and convert them into studio apartments. For example, there is a house located at: XXXX Norene Lane which has not been lived in for years. My idea is to encourage a realtor to buy the house and fix it up. I believe the house has 4 bedrooms and two full bathrooms. The property manager can rent each bedroom to a tenant for $400 a month. Each tenant will have their own bedrooms. Each tenant will be required to share the upstairs bathroom, the downstairs bathroom, the living room, the dining room, the kitchen, the laundry area in the basement and the basement. Of course, each property manager will be allowed to have their own rules and regulations.

I am aware there are both advantages and disadvantages. An advantage is with person will not be homeless. A disadvantage is except for the bedroom, each tenant will be required to share the rest of the house with others. But there are both pros and cons to everything.

An excellent place to turn into apartments is a former Church located at: XXXX Outer Loop Road. There are also several four-bedroom and two-bathroom houses throughout Newburg which can be converted into "dorm like" living quarters. Preferably, the tenants will be working adults.

For me, I would prefer to live in a "dorm like" living quarter than to be homeless or living in an over-crowded house.

I hope that converting big houses and big buildings into "dorm like" living quarters can be considered.

Thank you for reading my letter. I deeply appreciate it.

*I never received a response letter.

What Do You Want To Say?

I wrote and mailed this letter to the Louisville mayor, my state senator, and my state representative on May 16, 2020.

School Supplies Donation Boxes

Dear _____:

I am writing with another idea. I know Louisville is an amazing city filled with generous people. My idea is to encourage all the department stores and dollar stores to have a school supply donation box at the front of their stores. Store customers can be encouraged to put items in the box such as: notebooks, pencils, ink pens, erasers, packs of loose leaf paper, folders, backpacks, snacks, and so on. The items can be transported to the elementary or middle school closest to the store.

It was brought to my attention that teachers are required to buy their students' supplies and snacks. My idea is to encourage all the department stores and dollar stores to set up school supply donation boxes for school supply donations.

Thank you for reading my letter. I deeply appreciate it.

*Changes were made to this letter from the original letter.

*I do not remember receiving a response from anybody in office.

I wrote and mailed this letter to the CEOs of some major Department Store franchises on May 22, 2020.

Stores Collecting School Supplies

Dear _____:

I am writing with an idea. My idea is to encourage all your stores to collect donations for their elementary and middle schools. Once a week, a principal or assistant principal will pick up the items from the store. If the store in the 40218 zip code has a full box, then the principal or assistant principal from a school in the 40218 zip code will go to the store to pick up the donated items.

The items to be put into the school donation boxes can include notebooks, loose leaf paper, pencils, ink pens, tablets, calculators, glue, paste, erasers, pencil cases, backpacks, snacks, and other items of need.

It was recently brought to my attention that teachers are now required to buy their students' school supplies. I believe donated school supplies can help schoolteachers tremendously.

I hope the idea of collecting items for local schools can be discussed and considered.

Thank you for reading my letter. I deeply appreciate it.

I received a positive response from the contact center of a corporate office on June 4, 2020.

Dear Dorothea,

Thank you for taking the time to contact us regarding your suggestion. We are happy to help.

Our company strives to provide our customers with quality products at great prices to meet their needs and preferences. We want you to know that we have reviewed your letter and your comments have been shared with the appropriate team.

Each concern/issue we receive is very important to us and gives us the opportunity to improve upon the level of services our customers have come to expect. It is customers like you who help us continue to offer everyday low prices and friendly service. If you have any additional questions or would like to reach out to us for any further assistance, please call Customer Relations on contact: 1-800-XXX-XXXX. Should you like to respond to this letter, we politely request you provide a telephone number and/or email address, so we can respond as soon as possible. Thank you.

Your reference number is: XXXXXX-XXXXXX

Sincerely,

Customer Care

*The company's identity I choose to not reveal.

I received an second contact letter from another corporate office around December 18, 2020.

Dear Ms. Maddox,

I hope this letter finds you well. Thank you for your beautiful letter. We are pleased to let you know that we received your letter pertaining to collecting donations for the local schools in the Louisville, KY area. We have donated a $100 gift card to the XXXXXXX High School and XXXXXXX Middle School both near store #XXX so they can purchase supplies for their upcoming school semester. Thank you again for sharing your wonderful idea with us. Have a happy holiday.

Best regards,
(Name I choose to withhold)
Community Initiatives Coordinator
*Names and store location, I choose to not reveal.

I wrote and mailed this letter to the Louisville mayor, my state senator, and my state representative on May 28, 2020.

Idea for Children in Group Homes

Dear _____:

I am writing with another idea. My idea is to encourage children 16 or older who are in a group home to enlist in Job Corps. Some advantages are everything is free to them; they receive a high school diploma; and they receive free job training.

To encourage residents of group homes can also bring advantages to our city and state. Both the city of Louisville and the state of Kentucky will gain people to fill all the high demand jobs. For example, all the hospitals in Louisville are in desperate need of Nationally Certified Pharmacy Technicians. All the auto shops throughout Louisville are in desperate need of Certified Auto Repair Technicians. All the restaurant chains in Louisville are in desperate need of cooks. To encourage those 16 and older who live in group homes to enroll in Job Corps will be a great advantage to us too. If this sounds like a good idea, then you can contact Job Corps at:

Job Corps Placement Center

XXXX W. Broadway

Louisville, Ky. 40211

502-XXX-XXXX

I hope to let residents of group homes who are 16 or older to join Job Corps can be discusses and considered.

Thank you for reading my letter. I deeply appreciate it.

*Some changes were made to this letter from the original letter.

*I never received a response letter.

D. E. Maddox | 218

I wrote and mailed this letter to the Louisville mayor on (I believe) June 6, 2020.

A Local Food Bank

Dear Mayor _____:

I wrote to let you know Louisville is doing an outstanding job. There are Free Food Distribution and Free Food Pantries throughout the city. Louisville is an amazing city filled with amazing people. Also, I am not the only "military brat" who's glad to call Louisville "home." I know of some grocery stores who collect for the local food bank. My idea is to encourage <u>all</u> grocery stores throughout Louisville to collect for our local food bank. The donated items can include canned goods, other non-perishable items, snacks, and so on. Hopefully, some donated items can also include can openers, paper-plates, paper bowls, plastic eating utensils, and paper cups. Our local food bank is a great organization because they help people in our own city. In other words, they help us to help our neighbors. My idea is to encourage all grocery stores in Louisville to collect food items for our local food bank. If the items cannot be transported to the food bank on Fern Valley Road, then church leaders near the grocery stores can pick up the items and donate them to their church food pantry. For example, if a grocery store in West Louisville has a barrel full of donated items, then the churches near that grocery store can pick up the items to be distributed to those in the area who need food but have no money to buy food with as well as those who cannot leave their homes due to physical limitations. I know this would be a tremendous blessing to the elderly and disabled. I hope all grocery stores can be encouraged to participate in the local food bank donations. Thank you for reading my letter. I deeply appreciate it. *Name of food distribution organization I choose to not give. *I never received a response letter.

I wrote and mailed this letter to the Louisville mayor on June 13, 2020.

Free Food Pantry Boxes

Dear Mayor _____:

I am writing with another concern. My concern is for those who want to put a free food pantry box in front of their house. This isn't a good idea because if the box is empty, then the recipients might knock on the home-owners' doors asking for food. If the homeowners have no food to spare, then the recipients might say "thank you" and leave. But there are people who might get violent and demand food from the homeowners. To make matters worse, there are those who might force their way into the house and start looking for food.

A great idea is to never allow anybody to put food boxes in front of their houses. Doing this can lead to something bod happening to the homeowners. Free boxes can be put near churches or businesses—but not in front of houses.

Thank you for reading my letter. I deeply appreciate it.

*I never received a response letter.

I wrote and mailed this letter to the CEO of a restaurant franchise on June 21, 2020.

A Restaurant in a Southeast City

Dear _____CEO:

I am writing with a serious concern. Someone put a post on social media pertaining to a restaurant in a southeast city. The post states the dining room is opened to "Blacks Only." Many people find this post both offensive and racist!

I believe the "Blacks Only" post is fake. I posted a GIF of a woman saying, "Fake! Fake! Fake! Fake! Fake!" Others also said the post was "fake."

This post can damage your company's reputation. If this was posted as a "joke" then many of us see it as not funny!

Thank you for reading my letter. I deeply appreciate it.

*Name of location of restaurant I choose to not reveal.

*I never received a response letter.

_____

I wrote and mailed this letter to the Louisville mayor, my state senator, and my state representative on June 24, 2020.

To Have One Place to Vote

Dear _____:

I am writing with another concern. To have everybody in Louisville vote at only one place was a bad idea. I took my neighbor and myself to vote after I got off my 10-hour shift at work. My neighbor and I sat in traffic for more than one-and-a-half hours. I drove my father's car and fortunately for me there was one-quarter of a tank of gas. I believe some people ran out of gas. To make matters worse, there were so many inpatient drivers who nearly caused an accident. To have more than 100,000 voters come to one location is unrealistic.

It is not a good idea to have over 100,000 voters come to one location. My idea is to go back to the way it has been for decades. Have all the residents in Newburg vote at the elementary and middle schools closest to their homes. Have all the residents of West Louisville vote at the elementary and middle schools closest to their homes. Have all the residents in East Louisville vote at the elementary and middle schools closest to their homes. Have all the residents on the Okolona Area vote at the elementary and middle schools closest to their homes. If you want to open the fairgrounds to voters, then all the residents of Downtown Louisville and South Louisville vote there. I hope the idea of going back to how things used to be can be discussed and considered.

Thank you for reading my letter. I deeply appreciate it.

*I do not remember receiving a response letter.

I wrote and mailed this letter to the Inventor and CEO of a special kind of pillow on July 2, 2020. He also owns a pillow and bedding company.

Temperature Pillows

Dear _____:

I am writing with some ideas. If possible, can you produce temperature pillows? The head pillows can be slightly warm during the winter and slightly cool during the summer. I hope you can also produce full body pillows which can also be slightly warm during the winter and slightly cool during the summer. The one and only disadvantage to these pillows is they cannot get wet. You can wash the pillow covers, but not the pillows. Many people live on fixed incomes. This means they cannot run their air all summer long. Also, many people live in homes with neither central air nor central heat. Both the head pillows and body pillows are attended to keep consumers "warm" in the winter and "cool" in the summer. I hope those in deep need of these kinds of pillows can receive them from relatives, friends, neighbors, or church members as a birthday gift, Christmas gift or house-warming gift. The reason why I suggest these pillows be slightly warm during the winter or slightly cool during the summer is because I do not want anybody to "burn" themselves or get "front bite." I hope the temperature pillows (both head and full body pillows) can be made for both adults and children. I pray and hope these temperature pillows can be produced. I also pray and hope they can benefit consumers in more ways than I will ever know. Thank you for reading my letter. I deeply appreciate it.

Sincerely,

P.S. The temperature control will be sewn into the center of the pillow. The knobs to make the pillows warm or cold will be on the "back" of the pillows.

*Changes were made to this letter from the original letter.

*I never received a response letter.

What Do You Want To Say?

I wrote and mailed this letter to the Louisville mayor, my state senator, and my state representative on July 5, 2020.

A "No Knock" Law

Dear _____:

A friend of mine told me a story that really upsets me. My friend is 50 and is living in the same house he lived in since his parents brought him home from the hospital. He served nearly 30 years in the Army and has recently returned to Louisville. His parents are deceased, and he lives in the house. People knock on his door multiple times a month to ask him if he wants to sell his house. His answer is always "no."

It should be against the law to knock on the door to ask somebody if they want to sell their house. If possible, I hope Louisville can come up with a "No Knock" Law when it comes to solicitation of any kind. The only exceptions can be girls selling girl scout cookies and school-aged children selling candy bars. Besides that, it should be against the law to knock on anybody's door to ask them if they want to sell their house or buy anything or join a religious group or for political campaigns.

Many people prefer to never have strangers knock on their doors for solicitation purposes.

Thank you for reading my letter. I deeply appreciate it.

*I never received a response letter.

I wrote and mailed this letter to a few local property managers on July 5, 2020.

Property Managers

I am Dorothea Maddox, and I am writing with an idea. If any of your residents move out and leave behind unopened food that is not expired, the I will be glad to pick it up.

There are free food pantry boxes and libraries throughout Louisville. I will be glad to collect the "left behind" food and put it into a nearby food box. The food boxes are for those who need food but have no money to buy food. I try to buy food from stores when I can to put in the food boxes, but other financial obligations come up.

Please call me when tenants move out and leave food behind. Thank you for reading my letter. I deeply appreciate it.

Sincerely,

502-XXX-XXXX

*I never received a response letter. I did receive a phone call from a property manager who thought this was a great idea and wanted to set up a food box in her apartment complex.

I wrote and mailed this letter to the Internal Revenue Service (IRS) on July 7, 2020.

Stimulus Checks

To Whom It May Concern:

I am writing with a concern. It was brought to my attention that $4.5 billion worth of stimulus checks were mailed to deceased people. To make matters worse, many recipients threw stimulus checks in the garbage.

My idea it to make it a crime (criminal offense) to throw stimulus checks in the garbage. If the recipients are deceased, then the surviving relative, friend or caretaker should be required to write a note on the envelope which reads, "Return to Sender. Person is deceased." If the person does not want his or her stimulus check, then they are to write on the envelope, "Return to Sender."

To have $4.5 billion worth of stimulus checks sent to deceased people or thrown in the garbage is a terrible thing. The unneeded stimulus checks should be returned, recirculated, and sent to those who are still waiting to receive their stimulus checks.

Thank you for reading my letter. I deeply appreciate it.

*Some changes were made to this letter from the original letter.

*I never received a response letter.

I wrote and mailed this letter to a local church on July 19, 2020.

Free Food Box

Dear Senior Pastor:

I am writing with an idea. My idea is for the church to set up a food box in the grassy area behind the church.

Some of the advantages to having a food box are:

*If you have surplus food after a food distribution, then you can put it into the food box.

*If people in need of food cannot make it to the food distribution due to their work schedule of other obligations, then they can come to the box to get food at their convenience.

*Instead of people knocking on the door begging they can go to the food box to get food.

I am sure there are other advantages to having a food box at your church.

Both church members and community members can be encouraged to donate what they can to the food box. If a person can afford to only donate $10 worth of items, then they are doing what they can. May GOD reward them for doing what they can.

The motto of many food boxes is, "Take what you need. Give what you can." A person put a saying on one box that reads, "Please take for your needs. Never take for your greeds."

If you can do so, then the church can have their own rules for the box. For example, put a note on the box which reads, "This church is not responsible for any negative outcomes due to the consumption of the food or beverages in or around this box." If you have surveillance cameras on your property, then you can post warnings on (or near) the box indicating so.

Items which can be donated to the box can include:

*Non-perishable food items

*Beverages that do not need refrigeration

*Store-bought hygienic items such as soap, deodorant, toothpaste, feminine products, baby wipes, diapers, and so on

*Books that are in good condition

*Grocery bags

Items that cannot be donated are:

*Old, tattered clothes and shoes

*Used undergarments and socks

*Broken toys and other broken items

*Expired and/or rotting food as well as expired beverages

Anything that is in bad condition needs to be thrown in the garbage!

An advantage to having a box in the grassy area behind the Church is both donors and recipients have a safe place to park. A disadvantage is it is unwise for anybody to go to the box after dark time. I would suggest nobody tries to go to the box after dark.

Thank you for reading my letter. I deeply appreciate it.

Here is my phone number if you want to contact me, 502-XXX-XXXX.

*Changes were made to this letter from the original letter.

*I never received a response letter.

I wrote and mailed this letter to the CEO's of two parcel delivery service companies. I mailed the first letter on August 12, 2020 and the second letter on August 13, 2020.

Arcades

Dear CEO:

I am writing with an idea. I have heard of a city in California in which they have arcade games that simulate being an airplane pilot. In other words, the players are the "pilots" taking virtual trips. My idea is for your company to set up arcades throughout the United States in which young people can play virtual reality games in which they simulate being airplane pilots. These virtual reality games will inspire to become pilots in the future. These arcades can also have video virtual reality games that allow players to also simulate CDL Drivers. If possible, also have virtual reality games that simulate other career choices in your company.

When I was a teenager in the early 1980's, many pre-teens and teenagers spent lots of time at the arcades. My idea is for your company to establish arcades throughout the United States and have virtual reality games which simulate real careers at your company. After somebody graduates from high school, they can receive career training which leads to a great career.

All cities throughout the United States are in desperate need of airplane pilots and CDL drivers. Also, Louisville, Kentucky, and other cities are in desperate need of a variety of positions to be filled at your company.

Due to the Covid19 Pandemic, I am aware all the arcades will have strict guidelines to follow such as facemasks and social distancing being required.

I hope arcades can be established to inspire young people to establish a career at your company.

Thank you for reading my letter. I deeply appreciate it.

Sincerely,

P.S. Please share this letter with your parcel delivery service company offices throughout the United States. Thanks in advance.

*Changes were made to this letter from the original letter.

*I received a response a letter from the second company, but not the first company.

*The names of these companies I choose to not reveal.

The Director of a Parcel Delivery Service Company wrote and mailed this letter on September 25, 2020. I received this letter on September 28, 2020.

Dorothea,

Thank you for sharing your interesting idea about simulating our parcel delivery service company jobs in arcade-like games.

Interestingly, the company is starting to move in this direction with some of our online applications. The concept is called gamification, and it allows people to learn more about jobs before applying and to make the experience more enjoyable.

In addition, our parcel delivery service company will have interactive games, including a flight simulator, in a Kentucky Science Center exhibit set to open in October. We also underwrite virtual aviation and astronaut experiences at the Aviation Academy in West Louisville.

We appreciate your creative thinking and have shared your ideas.

Best Wishes,

(Hand-written signature of Director)

Airlines Strategic Communications Director

*Names I choose to not reveal.

What Do You Want To Say?

I wrote and mailed this letter to the CEO of a restaurant franchise on August 18, 2020.

Ideal Restaurant Location

Dear Manager:

I am writing with an idea. If you are interested in a second restaurant in Louisville, Kentucky, then there are vacant buildings on Outer Loop Road. A great location used to be a restaurant which was recently shut down. The location is: XXXX Outer Loop Road/ Louisville, Ky. 402XX. Hopefully, another restaurant can also be located on Fern Valley Road near industrial sites. Either Outer Loop Road or Fern Valley Road would be a great location for another restaurant.

I hope to see another restaurant in Louisville soon.

Thank you for reading my letter. I deeply appreciate it.

Sincerely

*Changes were made to this letter from the original letter.

*Locations and name of restaurant I choose to not reveal.

*I never received a response letter.

I wrote and mailed this letter to the Louisville mayor, my state senator, and my state representative on August 29, 2020.

Prospective Drive-In Location

Dear _____:

I am writing with another idea. There is a vacant building which is located at: XXXX Preston Highway. This used to be a fitness center, but it is now a vacant retail building. My idea is to turn this vacant retail building into a drive-in. People will get to enjoy movies while practicing social distancing. The drive-in can also be used to view local events such as the Kentucky Derby and Thunder Over Louisville. Of course, the drive-in will need a fence that is at least 10 feet high to prevent people from sneaking in without paying. I know people who are local filmmakers. I would also encourage them to produce material at this drive-in. The drive-in can show matinees as well as movies at night. The popcorn and other refreshments can be sold at a small building on the other side of the drive-in screen.

The location is next to a restaurant. A family can have dinner at the restaurant and then go to a movie after dinner. This would be a great idea for those on dates. This area is 50,400 square feet which means there will be plenty of places to park. If possible, add a play area for small children. I hope to put a drive-in at: XXXX Preston Highway, in South Central Louisville, can be discussed and taken into consideration. Thank you for reading my letter. I deeply appreciate it.

Sincerely,

Dorothea Maddox

P.S. This can also bring back tourism.

*Names and locations to choose to not reveal.

*I never received a response letter.

I wrote and mailed this letter to the "Right to Life" group on October 2, 2020.

Abortions' Impact on Louisville, Kentucky

To Whom It May Concern:

I am writing a letter pertaining to the impact of abortions on Louisville, Kentucky.

Currently, Louisville, Kentucky has more "Now Hiring" signs than ever before. We literally have way more jobs than people to fill them. Our city is short-handed everywhere. To make matters worse, our nation is short-handed when it comes to the United States military. There are military personnel who are forced to serve 9 or 11 or 13 tours of duty overseas due to not having enough people in the United States military. According to my father, this nation has experienced 10 holocausts since Roe Vs. Wade in 1973. As a result, this nation is short-handed when it comes to high-demand careers as well as our United States military. Louisville is not the only place in Kentucky impacted by their high number of abortions. There is a restaurant in Simpsonville (Shelby County) which had to be shut down due to nobody being available to work there. My idea is to put adoption billboards near abortion clinics. Hopefully, there are couples who want to adopt babies of any race or ethnicity.

Just like most other cities, Louisville is in desperate need of doctors, surgeons, surgical technicians, pharmacists, Nationally Certified Pharmacy Technicians, auto repair technicians, school bus drivers, CDL drivers, school teachers, substitute teachers, nurses, and so on. Abortion was legalized in 1973. Starting in the early 1990's, military recruitment began to decline a great deal. Who is going to fight to protect us if we do not have enough people in our military to do so? I know of a woman who was in her mid-

50's when she was required to serve a final "tour of duty" on Iraq due to not enough young people serving in our military. That makes no sense!

There are also private schools here in Louisville that had to shut down due to low attendance. In other words, there are not enough people to enroll. I highly encourage wealthy couples to adopt babies of any race or ethnicity. I even encourage couples to stand in front of abortion clinics with signs that read, "Give us the baby. We'll raise the baby."

Thank you for reading my letter. I deeply appreciate it.

Sincerely,

Dorothea Maddox

*Some changes were made to this letter from the original one.

This response letter was hand-written and mailed on October 14, 2020. I received it on October 19, 2020.

Dear Ms. Dorothea Maddox

Thank you so much for your kind note.

It is sad to hear of how your hometown of Louisville has been impacted. I think often of the many couples that I know personally who struggle with infertility. They would love to adopt a local child, but often resort to expensive overseas adoption.

I am grateful that my parents, clearly like yours, raised me to see the sadness and harm of abortion. Your father is a smart man.

We had our 2014 National Right to Life Convention in Louisville, Ky. I believe there was another there earlier as well. Unfortunately, this year's was cancelled, but next year it will be in Herndon, Va., just outside D.C. We would love more pro-lifers like your father and yourself to join us! If you are interested there will be more information soon.

We do not send out physical mailings as often, so if you would like to be on our email list as well you can sign up at: _____.

Again, thank you for taking the time to write and for your support of the unborn.

Best,

(Hand-written signature)

What Do You Want To Say?

I also wrote and mailed this letter to the "Right to Life" group on October 2, 2020.

National Right to Life Letter

To Whom It May Concern:

I am writing with an idea. As a way of raising money to help those mothers who chose to have their babies, the National Right to Life group can sell face masks and bandannas which read "Pro-Life" or "Choose Life." The masks for babies and toddlers can read, "My Life Matters" or "All Lives Matter." The proceeds from the selling of the masks and bandannas can help mothers provide for their children, pay for child care, and provide job training. The proceeds can also be used to help fathers be real fathers and not be the kind of men who need other in society to raise, feed, and financially support their children for them. Hopefully, both parents can even receive vocational training to establish good-paying and "essential" careers.

Thank you for reading my letter. I deeply appreciate it.

Sincerely,

A response letter was written and mailed on October 29, 2020. I received the letter on October 31, 2020.

Response Letter

Dear Dorothea,

I am so sorry that it has taken so long to respond to your letter on October 10. As you imagine, the election and our voter activities have kept us all very busy in the post month.

Thank you so much for your idea about masks and bandannas. We are not usually in the field of producing apparel (we have, but it can be quite undertaking), but I have passed your idea along to other members of our team for consideration.

Thank you again for your letter. God bless you for your dedication to defending and protecting His most defenseless children.

For Life,

(Name I choose to not reveal)

Chief Marketing Officer

or

What Do You Want To Say?

I wrote and mailed this letter to the Louisville mayor, the Kentucky governor, my state senator, and my state representative in the middle of October.

Legalizing Marijuana for Medical Purposes

Dear _____:

I am writing about another concern and an idea. My concern is for those who need marijuana for medical reasons. For example, some people need marijuana for their glaucoma or to increase their appetites. Some people even need medical marijuana because they are receiving chemotherapy for cancer. The marijuana alleviates the side effects of the chemo treatments.

I was recently watching a comedy movie in which a woman carried her medical marijuana card with her as proof that it is legal for her to smoke marijuana. In a scene when other senior citizens were running away from the police officers, she was chasing the police officers to show them her medical marijuana card. My idea is to make it a requirement for all of those who need marijuana for medical reasons to buy a card. The card can cost $20 a year, or they can pay $1,000 for a lifetime "no expiration" date card. The money from the legal marijuana card purchases can add money to our state's economy. I hope the idea to legalize marijuana for medical purposes can be discussed and considered.

Thank you for reading my letter. I deeply appreciate it.

*This was written from the original letter to the best of my memory.

This response letter was written and mailed on October 30, 2020. I received the letter on November 2, 2020.

Dear Ms. Maddox:

Thank you for you continued input on issues important to you. I have recently read over your letter on Medical

Marijuana, and it interested me. You should know that I have been pushing for medical marijuana legalization since I have been in office. Progress had been made and passed in the house this year, I am hopeful it will pass this next year. Thank you again for your correspondence.

Sincerely,

(Signature)

State Representative

*I also received a "Kentucky General Assembly Compliments of state representative" card.

What Do You Want To Say?

I wrote and mailed this letter to the CEO of a dollar store franchise. I wrote the letter on November 11, 2020. I mailed it on November 12, 2020.

An Idea for the $5 off Purchase Receipts

Dear _____:

I am writing with another idea. The store customers receive receipts which allow us to get $5 off purchases of $25 or more, and it is for Saturdays only. My idea is to allow the coupon to be for the next seven days. For example, if I purchase items on Friday the 13th, then I will get a $5 off coupon which I can use between the 14th and 20th. In this case, the receipt can read as follows:

"$5 off $25 or more. To be used within seven days of date on receipt."

If I get the receipt on the 13th, then I must use it by the 20th.

Not everybody is able to get to the store on Saturdays due to other obligations. Some people, for example, work every Saturday. Some people babysit relatives' children every Saturday. The point is: not everyone can get to the store on Saturdays due to other obligations.

I hope you can make the $5 off $25 or more receipts good for the next 7 days.

Thank you for reading my letter. I deeply appreciate it.

*I never received a response letter.

I wrote and mailed this letter to a Store Manager of a local dollar store. I also wrote this letter on November 11, 2020, and mailed it on November 12, 2020.

Idea for a Store Manager

Dear Store Manager:

I am writing with an idea. I know that a nearby church has a free little library box. My idea is to encourage the church Leaders to also turn it into a food pantry box. You can also encourage customers to buy items to donate to the food pantry box. I also know your store had over 2,000 items that cost $1.00 or less. If possible, you can post the location of the pantry box on the store window or at the cash register. Hopefully, customers will be able to buy items to donate to the pantry box.

I hope the idea of customers being encouraged to buy and donate items to a pantry box can be discussed and considered.

Thank you for reading my letter. I deeply appreciate it.

*I never receive a response letter.

I wrote and mailed this letter to some grocery franchises on November 28, 2020.

Having Special Holiday Sales for Entire Month

Dear _____:

I am writing with an idea. During special holidays allow sales on <u>all</u> holiday food items for that entire month. For example, have discounts on hams and turkeys during the entire month of November for Thanksgiving celebrations. Have discounts during the entire month of December for Christmas holiday celebrations. Also, have discounts throughout the month of April for Easter celebrations. Many people are not able to have Thanksgiving dinner on Thanksgiving Day, or Christmas dinner on Christmas day or Easter dinner on Easter day due to work schedules, military deployment, family conflicts or other reasons. As a child, I was not allowed to have Thanksgiving dinner on Thanksgiving Day with my maternal grandparents because my mother's third husband never knew my twin brother and I existed, and she needed to keep us a "secret" from her third husband. Some people are not allowed to have Thanksgiving dinner on Thanksgiving Day or Christmas dinner on Christmas day or Easter dinner on Easter day with their families because their stepparent does not want them there. The family then needs to make other arrangements for the family member (or members) who is not wanted there on that day. Some people might have an uncle or aunt or cousin who does not want a specific family member at family events for reason we do not know about. The specific family member can celebrate Thanksgiving dinner or Christmas dinner or Easter dinner on another day. To have discounts the entire month will be a tremendous help on those who host two or more holiday dinners each holiday season due to various family circumstances. It is amazing how some people cannot attend family dinners due to their parentage or ancestry or disability or who they married (or some other reason).

To have discounts the entire month will be a tremendous help for those who host two or more holiday dinners each holiday due to various family circumstances.

I hope to have discounts on food for holiday celebrations can be active throughout the entire months of November, December, and April.

Thank you for reading my letter. I deeply appreciate it.

*Changes were made to this letter from the original one.

*I never received a response letter from anybody.

What Do You Want To Say?

I wrote and mailed this letter on the Kentucky governor, the Louisville mayor, my state senator, and my state representative on December 13, 2020.

Making People Order Services in Person

Dear _____:

Merry Christmas and Happy Holidays. I am writing about another concern. Many people are using other people's names and dates of birth to get phone services, cash loans, cable, and other services.

Fictional Scenario:

Suzy Que* and I were roommates who shared a house many years ago. While I was sleeping one night, she got into my purse and got some information about me. After I move out of the house, I begin to get bills for services I never ordered. I later found out that Suzy Que got all these services over the phone while using my name, date of birth, and social security number. To make matters worse, I am getting bills for services I never ordered.

My idea is to make it a requirement for all individuals to go to a company in person to receive services. If possible, allow an employee to come to the prospective customer's home to sign them up for services. The prospective customer is required to have their photo ID and social security card. If Suzy Que is not able to get phone service or cable service or some other service due to her limited income or her having a minimum wage job, then that is her problem. It should be against the law for anybody to obtain services over the phone. All services should be received in person. It is not fair for me to get bills for services I never signed up for because Suzy Que obtained services over the phone (or computer) using my name and date of birth. If anybody is the company is also involved in this fraud, then I will sue the company. For example, if a money transaction company allows Suzy Que to use my identity to get and receive money, then I should be able to sue the money transaction company. If a loan company allows Suzy Que to make loans using my identity, then I will sue the loan company.

All services should be obtained by all individuals in person. Never over the phone or computer.

Thank you for reading my letter. I deeply appreciate it.

*Suzy Que is a fictional person.

*Changes were made to this letter from the original one.

*I never received a response letter.

What Do You Want To Say?

I wrote and mailed this letter to the Louisville mayor, the Kentucky governor, my state senator, and my state representative on December 14, 2020.

Dear _____:

Merry Christmas and Happy Holidays. I am writing with another idea.

My idea is to require restaurants throughout Louisville (I said Kentucky for the Kentucky governor) to have drive-up windows. The only exception should be food courts in malls and restaurants on top floors of buildings.

The Covid19 Pandemic has put many restaurants out of business. To make matters worse, this put 1,000s of people out or work. The restaurants with drive-up windows are the restaurants which stayed busy and "open for business" during this pandemic. This pandemic is the reason why so many "sit down" restaurants with no drive-up window shut down.

Except for food courts in malls and restaurants on top floors, all restaurants in Louisville (I said Kentucky for the Kentucky governor) should have drive-up windows. This can prevent more restaurants from being forced to shut down due to pandemics.

Thank you for reading my letter. I deeply appreciate it.

*I never received a response letter.

I wrote and mailed this letter to some church leaders on December 29, 2020.

Dear Pastor _____:

I am writing with a serious concern. It was brought to my attention that people are knocking on doors to ask homeowners if they want to sell their house. If the homeowners let them in, then the scammers "scope" the house looking for items of value. The homeowners are later burglarized.

If strangers know on anybody's door, then I encourage the homeowner to look out their front window and shout, "Go away!" Even if the stranger is nicely dressed and/or has a name badge. The name badge might be bogus. If the stranger refuses to leave, then the homeowner can threaten to call the Police. I know the Police want people to call them if a stranger is at their door and refuse to leave.

Please warn everyone you know. Please warn all the people in your congregation. I want everyone in our community to be safe in 2021. Thanks in advance.

*I never received a response letter.

*Changes were made to this letter from the original one.

I wrote and mailed this letter to a local community center on January 19, 2021.

Setting Up a Free Food/Book Box

To Whom It May Concern:

I am Dorothea Maddox, and I am writing with an idea. If you can, then you can set up a free Food and Book Pantry Box in front of the community center. You can put surplus food and beverages as well as unwanted books in the box. My mom and I try to donate food and books to boxes when we can.

The purpose of a Free Food and Book Pantry Box is so recipients can come by to get food at their convenience. For example, if a person works 8am to 4:30pm and they work in Downtown Louisville, then they can come to the box after work to get food. Some people might work 10 to 12 hours a day, Monday thru Friday. They can come to the box on

Saturdays or Sundays to get food. Residents from the local Community can also be encouraged to donate food, drinks, and unwanted books to the box. I am aware the Boys' and Girls' Club down the street also has a pantry box. If their box becomes too full, then those of us who choose to donate food can come to the box in front of the community center to put in food. Many of the pantry boxes around the city have a motto that goes, "Take what you need. Give what you can." One box somewhere has a sign that read, "Please take for your needs. Please don't take for your greeds." Other signs read, "Please take what you need and leave something for somebody else in need."

If you choose to set up a box in front of the center, then you can post a sign that reads:

"Please take what you need."

"Nobody will judge you."

"Nobody will ask you what area you live in."

"Nobody will interrogate you."

As a volunteer, I came up with three rules for myself to live by:

#1—I will not judge.

#2—I will not ask anybody what area they live in.

#3—I will not interrogate any of the recipients.

For example, I will <u>never</u> ask any of the recipients, "Why are you unable to buy food from a grocery store?"

I hope a box can be set up in front of the community center soon.

Thank you for reading my letter. I deeply appreciate it.

*Changes were made to this letter from the original one.

*I never received a response letter.

What Do You Want To Say?

I wrote and mailed this letter on February 10, 2021. I wrote this letter to the local Sewer District Offices.

Trees in Jeopardy of Falling During an Ice Storm

To Whom It May Concern:

I am Dorothea Maddox, and I am writing with a serious concern. There are trees in the Newburg area that are in jeopardy of falling during a strong ice storm. Some of these trees are located behind 5401, 5403, 5405, 5407, and 5409 XXXXX Drive. The area behind our houses is public property. Some of these trees are also located along XXXXXXXXX Road, between XXXXXX Drive and Poplar Level Road. As far as the trees on XXXXXXXXX Road are concerned, there is always a possibility of a tree falling on a person. People walk on the sidewalk on XXXXXXXXX Road all hours of the night and day. I hope this never happens.

I hope somebody from the Sewer District Office can do something about all these trees. I hope these trees can be cut down to prevent any tragic occurrences.

Thank you for reading my letter. I deeply appreciate it.

*Some street locations I choose to not reveal.

*My parents received cards in the mail stating that people from their office will investigate the situation.

I wrote and mailed this letter to a local church on February 13, 2021.

People Feeling Intimidated about Receiving Food from Food Boxes.

Dear Pastors:

I am writing for two reasons. I want to say, "Thank you" for your food distributions and your food pantry box. I also want to discuss a serious concern. There are hungry people who (I believe) feel intimidated about receiving food from food boxes. Some people believe that somebody they know will see them and gossip about them. The question that goes through my mind is, "How many people in our area are going hungry because they feel intimidated about taking food from a food box?" I asked another person what she would suggest. She suggests that we put notes on the food boxes that read, "Thank you for letting us help you." I believe this is an excellent suggestion.

Do you have any suggestions about what we can do or say so those in need do not feel intimidated about getting food from food boxes?

A word of wisdom for those who are gossiping about the recipients is, "You better hope that you're never in a situation in which you need food from a local food pantry box."

Thank you for reading my letter. I deeply appreciate it.

*I never received a response letter.

I wrote this letter on March 19, 2021 and mailed it on March 20, 2021. I mailed letters to the Louisville mayor, my state senator, and my state representative.

Putting Speed Bumps on our Streets.

Dear _____:

I am writing with another concern. We need speed bumps on both XXXXXXX Boulevard and XXXXX Drive. People come speeding down our streets all hours of the night. Many years ago, a driver sped down XXXXXXX Boulevard and made "donuts" in the curve where XXXXXXX Boulevard and XXXXX Drive meet. This driver nearly hit my car!

I know that speed bumps will decrease the amount of speeding on both streets. There are nights when a vehicle would speed down XXXXXXX Boulevard towards our house and I would wonder if the driver will run their vehicle into our house.

I hope speed bumps can be installed on both XXXXXXX Boulevard and XXXXX Drive.

Thank you for reading my letter. I deeply appreciate it.

*Names of streets I choose to not reveal.

*Changes were made to this letter from the original one.

*I have not received a response letter yet.

In the 1990's and 2000's, some people in office lost loved ones while they were in office. I sent some of these individuals this poem.

YOU'RE GONE AWAY

I am a lonely one.

I feel like the only one.

I do not have you here to look to.

You are gone away.

Never to return one day.

I will always remember you.

Although I may never understand.

Only GOD above knows the plan.

Your memories will remain so true.

You are gone away.

Never to return one day.

Yet you left me sad and blue.

I have cried so many tears,

Enough to last so many years.

You left without telling why.

You are gone away.

Never to return one day.

I have no more tears left to cry.

Your photo, I hold so near.

In my heart, I hold you dear.

I deeply miss you being here.

You are gone away.

Never to return one day.

My memory of you remains so clear.

I am so sad and blue.

I am sad the whole day through.

Since I do not have you here to look to.

You are gone away.

Never to return one day.

I will always cherish you.

*Some people sent me responses and others never did.

Epilogue

I wrote so many more letters in the past and will continue to write more letters in the future. I try my best to write letters about issues that concern many of us in our areas. Not only do I write letters about social concerns and suggestions. I also send Christmas cards to people in office. Back in 2020, it was brought to my attention that the spouse of a person in office had the corona virus, and I sent a "get well" card to their spouse. If a person in office experiences a death in the family while in office, then I send them a condolence card. I even sent poems to some people in office who lost loved ones while they were in office.

I encourage others to write letters in which will bring positive changes in the world around us. For example, if your street needs speed bumps to stop speeders from speeding on your streets all hours of the night, then write a letter to your city mayor, your state senator, and your state representative. You can also encourage others to do the same. Even get a petition going if you have. The point is: for things to get better, we must be the ones to do something!

The one rule I learned to live by is, "If I have an idea and no power to do anything about it, then share that idea with somebody who does have the power to do something about it."

The Bible says that "Faith without works is dead." I pray all the time and I have faith that things will change. But I use my letter writing campaign as my "works."

About the Author

I was born in Watertown, New York. My father is Mr. John Maddox and was a staff sergeant in the Air Force and my birth mother was Mr. Ruth (Geer) Maddox. I also have a twin brother named Mr. John Francis Maddox. We were born on October 26, 1968. I lived in Pulaski, New York until my brother and I were 10 months old. From there, we moved to Crete, Greece. We lived there until we were 2 years old and then we moved to Fort Meade, Maryland. We lived there until we were 5 years old and then moved to Fort Ord, California. After leaving California, we lived in Louisville, Kentucky with an aunt for until July, 1975. We lived in Okinawa, Japan from July, 1975 until January, 1978. My twin brother and I stayed in Bloomfield, Kentucky with our paternal grandparents from January, 1978 until August, 1978. We returned to Fort Meade in August, 1978 and stayed there until my father retired from the Air Force in June, 1983. I spend a year in Bloomfield, Kentucky and a year in Severn, Maryland. I returned to Louisville, Kentucky in August, 1985 and I've lived in Kentucky ever since. I graduated from Moore High School in 1987 and then attended Kentucky State University. I never graduated. In

2006, I attended Daymar College and graduated with a Pharmacy Technology Degree. I now work at Kentucky Central Fill-Kroger Pharmacy. I've been employed there for over 12 years. I have a daughter named Myra and 2 grandsons, Kaleb and Noah. Also, my stepmother is Mrs. Darcy Maddox. They got married on November 7, 1980 when we were living in Fort Meade, Maryland. Darcy has been in my life since my brother and I were 12.

For more information regarding D. E. Maddox, email at thea_maddox@yahoo.com.

www.ingramcontent.com/pod-product-compliance
Lightning Source LLC
Chambersburg PA
CBHW071518160426
43196CB00010B/1567